THE ALICE CRIMMINS CASE

50 STATES of CRIME NEW YORK

THE ALICE CRIMMINS CASE

ANAÏS RENEVIER
TRANSLATED BY LAURIE BENNETT

CRIME INK

NEW YORK

THE ALICE CRIMMINS CASE

Crime Ink
An Imprint of Penzler Publishers
58 Warren Street
New York, N.Y. 10007

Edited by Elsa Delachair and Stéphane Régy.
© Editions 10/18, Département d'Univers Poche, 2023
In association with So Press/Society
English translation copyright: © 2025 by Laurie Bennett

First Crime Ink edition

Cover design by Charles Perry, inspired by the French language
edition cover design by Nicolas Caminade

Interior design by Maria Fernandez

Library of Congress Control Number: 2024919428

ISBN: 978-1-61316-629-1
eBook ISBN: 978-1-61316-630-7

10 9 8 7 6 5 4 3 2 1

Printed in the United States of America
Distributed by W. W. Norton & Company

To my parents.
To Anna Blume.

Contents

THE DISAPPEARANCE

1

The Baby Carriage Beneath the Window

The alarm clock brought her back to reality with a jolt, signaling the end of a short night and a return to her daily routine. On the morning of July 14, 1965, at 8:30, Alice Crimmins awoke to a quiet apartment, disturbed only by the hum of her air-conditioning unit.

First step: hair and makeup. Before going to check on her children in the room across the hall, before walking Brandy, their Pomeranian, the young mother always saved a few minutes for herself. She teased her thick strawberry-blonde hair, pulling it into an elegant bouffant. She caked her pale face in foundation, daubed a touch of blush onto her cheekbones, and finished with a stroke of eyeliner to bring out her light, almond-shaped eyes. Now her day could begin.

She noticed something odd in the apartment—a heavy silence. By this time of the morning, she could usually hear the voices of her children, five-year-old Eddie Jr. and his four-year-old sister Missy, filling their home. Today, there was nothing but silence. Alice crossed the hall and opened the door to their room. Both beds were empty. The casement window was wide open and the screen, which Alice had installed the day before, was gone. She found it leaning against the wall outside, near a baby carriage the building super used as a cart.

The apartment was on the ground floor, in the Kew Gardens Hills neighborhood. Between the window and the street stood only a manicured patch of lawn and a wide, tidy sidewalk. Around these parts, everything looked the same. The three-story red-brick building in which Alice and her children lived was a mirror image of the adjoining units. Across the street stood an exact replica of this model. Same bricks, same lawn, same walkway. The pattern was reflected in the surrounding blocks, fanning out endlessly, in a vast, red iron-oxide monochrome.

The uniformity left no room for whimsy. On either side of the thin walls, working-class families rented two- or three-bedroom apartments and led uneventful lives, identical to those of their neighbors. Fathers worked as laborers or civil servants, mothers as housewives or sales-clerks. When residents crossed paths, their interactions were cordial but rarely friendly. No one settled in this part of Queens hoping to spend their life here.

On paper, this was New York, but it felt far from Manhattan, which everyone here called "The City." Kew Gardens Hills existed halfway between urban frenzy and suburban tranquility. It was a transitional place, where people stayed after the birth of their youngest child and until their next promotion, until they could afford a piece of the American Dream: their own house with their own little yard.

As the neighbors walked past the Crimminses' building on their way to work, they usually glanced at the children's bedroom window. Perched on the sill, the children would wave at people as they walked by. Eddie Jr. and Alice were named after their parents, but everyone called the little girl Missy. Some days, they would sneak out to play on the lawn in front of the building while their mother was still sleeping.

But this morning, they were neither in their room nor at the window nor on the lawn. Alice first assumed they'd slipped out to sweet-talk a neighbor into giving them pancakes or some kind of treat. She checked in with several of them. Among these neighbors was

Theresa Costello, one of the children's babysitters. Though in the middle of breakfast when Alice arrived, the fourteen-year-old dropped everything to help with the search. But after a quick walk through the area, there was still no sign of Eddie and Missy. Shortly after 9:00 A.M., Alice decided to do the one thing she had been hoping to avoid: She called the children's father.

The Crimmins couple, twenty-six-year-old Alice and twenty-nine-year-old Eddie Sr., had been separated for a year and a half. Although they were not yet divorced, Eddie had moved out of the family's home at Alice's request. The troubles had begun after Missy's birth. It was an age-old, rather ordinary tale: the husband starts to go out often, the wife criticizes him for leaving her alone, frustration builds, and arguments become heated. Alice started seeing lovers.

In the final months before their separation, the two would sometimes go for weeks without speaking, even attending dinners with friends—together—where they would not utter a single word to each other for the entire evening. But living apart did nothing to help the situation. Two weeks earlier, Eddie had officially filed for custody of the children, and ever since, the Crimmins couple had been at war, a battle consisting of furious phone calls and letters from lawyers. To settle the matter, a court hearing had been scheduled for the coming Monday.

Eddie awoke to his phone ringing.

"Eddie? Have you got the kids?"

"No."

"Eddie, don't play games with me!"

"I don't have them."

"Eddie, don't fool around! Please don't do this to me!"

Despite years of anger, conflicts, and accusations, Eddie could hear the panic in Alice's voice and went over to her apartment immediately. It was his idea to make the next call. At 9:44 A.M., the phone rang at the local precinct. "My name is Crimmins, Eddie Crimmins. My children are missing . . ."

Detective Gerard Piering's day began at the Queens Criminal Courthouse, where he was waiting to testify in the trial of a burglar he'd arrested some time ago. As fate would have it, the hearing was postponed, and Piering called the precinct to get an update on current cases. Two children, aged four and five, had gone missing. Their home was just a short drive from the courthouse, so off he went to investigate the disappearance.

When he reached Alice Crimmins's home at roughly 10:30 A.M., Piering was the first detective on the scene. He took a quick look around. In the children's room, a small bed was against the left wall, with a crib along the right wall. Between the two beds, a bureau had been placed under the window. There was also a metal armoire and a toy chest. Nothing seemed out of place; there were no signs of a struggle, no mess.

But a few details bothered the detective. First, a latch had been installed on the outside of the bedroom door. The parents explained that little Eddie would sometimes raid the refrigerator at night, so this was the solution they'd come up with to save him the upset stomach. That meant the children were locked in at night. Second, Piering noticed a dozen empty liquor bottles in the kitchen garbage can. The children's mother told him that she'd been planning to throw them away, as she was expecting a visit from a court agent related to the custody suit and had cleaned the house thoroughly in the days prior. She had even repainted the foyer.

Despite the explanations, Gerard Piering did not like what he was seeing in the apartment and—above all—he did not like the woman standing before him.

To Piering, a thirty-five-year-old policeman and father of six, Alice did not fit the image of a worried mother. She wore canary-yellow toreador pants, a colorful blouse, and black ballet flats. Her eyes were heavily made up. Behind an impenetrable gaze, she seemed to harbor a fiery inner passion and so many mysteries. He couldn't help but notice that she didn't shed a single tear. As the children's mother answered his questions, her voice was smooth, her attitude nonchalant. He could make out a light accent carried over from the Bronx, where she had grown up. Languidly, she picked up a cigarette and asked the detective for a light. Piering felt his hackles rise. Her children were missing, and this woman was looking for a match?

Piering and the other police officers on the scene soon made another discovery: Under Alice Crimmins's bed, they found a box of letters and cards, including restaurant menus signed by politicians. The mementos featured names like Robert Wagner, the mayor of New York, and even Senator Robert Kennedy, the brother of President John Fitzgerald Kennedy, who had been assassinated two years earlier. Not exactly what you would expect to find in the home of a twenty-six-year-old woman working as a waitress in a few local bars. Her husband was a mechanic at JFK Airport, where he worked the night shift.

Both parents seemed to lead ordinary lives in a modest part of Queens. In their world, encounters with Manhattan's high society were rare. When asked to explain herself, Alice told detectives that she'd had brief encounters with these men at social events to which she'd been invited. Soon, more secrets were pulled from the box under the bed. Alice had kept letters from her paramours, who often nicknamed her "Rusty."

To Detective Piering, the contents of the box were an affront to his deeply held moral values. In the world of this fervent Catholic, wives did not kick their husbands to the curb. They did not drink alcohol. They did not attend lavish parties. And they certainly did not take lovers. Thus, when his colleague, Detective George Martin, finally arrived, Piering suggested they conduct two separate interrogations. He already knew whom he'd be taking care of. "You take Eddie, I'll take the bitch."

The parents were questioned at length about their where-abouts and actions in the previous day.

Alice Crimmins stated that on Tuesday, July 13, 1965, she ate breakfast with her children. Then, in the early afternoon, the three of them piled into her slightly dented Mercury convertible to enjoy the beautiful sunny day. They headed for Kissena Park, which was about a mile from home, and picked up food for a picnic along the way. In the park, Eddie and Missy played for hours, spending a little time on the swings with their mother and playing games on the grass with friends. The simple pleasures of summer and childhood.

On the drive back, the children's mother stopped at a pay phone to call her attorney, then bought groceries for dinner. She served the meal, defrosted veal, at 7:30 P.M. The three of them then went back out for a short drive. Alice admitted that this evening outing had mostly been an excuse to locate her husband's vehicle, as he also lived in the neighborhood.

Her lawyer had quietly suggested that she might glean information about him in this way, or come across a compromising detail, perhaps proof of a lover. Who knew? It could help her case at the custody hearing. So she drove through the neighborhood while the children horsed around in the back seat. Alice Crimmins found nothing. Before going home, she made one last stop for gas at roughly 8:30 P.M., as far as she could recall.

Eddie Crimmins told the police that Tuesday was his day off. In his narrative of the day, he had gotten up at dawn to practice his golf swing and enjoy the fresh morning air on the green. Like Alice, he confessed that he later spent several hours attempting to locate his wife's convertible. He, too, had been hoping to find incriminating evidence to show in court.

Eddie had been aware of Alice's extramarital adventures for some time now. And he couldn't stand it. That's why he'd gone to Huntington, Long Island, twenty-five miles from Queens, to stake out the luxurious home of one of Alice's lovers. But Eddie had found no sign of his wife there. He spent the next few hours drowning his sorrows in a few beers while watching the Mets on TV. He had nothing else to say.

Theresa Costello, the young neighbor, was the last nonfamily member to have seen, or rather heard, the children. At approximately 8:30 P.M., on her way to a babysitting job, she had passed by their window and overheard snippets of a conversation. She recognized Alice's voice, telling the little ones to pray. Theresa said she clearly heard Missy say, "God bless Mommy and Daddy." She also remembered another detail: The super's cart, a converted baby carriage, had not been there when she walked by in the evening.

Detectives now wanted to know how the parents had spent their time after dark.

According to Alice Crimmins, on the night her children went missing, she woke them up around midnight to take them to the bathroom. Missy mumbled that she didn't want to get up. Eddie followed his mother like a sleepwalker, barely awake. Alice also took the dog out several times, chipped away at the apartment cleanup, and eventually put her feet up to watch TV.

The night was punctuated by several phone calls, evidence of her amorous pursuits. First, she dialed up a bar in the Bronx, where one of her beaus went every Tuesday night. When she offered to join him, he declined, telling her he was about to head home. A little later, it was Alice's turn to get a call. It was a different companion, the man from Huntington. This time, the roles were reversed; he was at a bar with his cousin and asked if she cared to join them. And this time, she declined the invitation. She didn't really care to see him and pretended that she'd be unable to find a sitter so late.

A few miles away, Eddie Crimmins was eating pizza for dinner in front of the TV. And although he was an avid beer drinker, he did something quite unusual—he went out for gin and tonics, ordering his last drink a little before three o'clock in the morning. On his way home, Eddie made one final stop and parked at the back of Alice's building. He often came here to spy on her. Sitting in the shadows of the parking lot, he would stare at the home from which he had been banished. That evening, he noticed the lights were on in both the living room and bedroom.

When he made it back to his place, Eddie called his wife to talk about a former maid who claimed Alice owed her $600. The discussion became heated. Yes, said Alice, she owed the woman money, but $150 at most. Eddie threatened his wife: If the maid didn't get her money soon, she would side with him and testify against Alice at the custody hearing. His wife brushed him off and suggested he talk to the maid himself, since he seemed to know her so well. Neither spouse had trouble admitting that these midnight calls were commonplace in their marriage. They took turns spewing their bitterness, fueled by seven stormy years of marriage.

"And then what happened?" the detectives asked Alice.

After hanging up, she took a bath, then went to bed at about four in the morning. Her husband said he watched a movie and then went to bed at the same time.

❖

Detectives were piecing together a picture of this family's home life, and they soon developed a theory. One of the parents had played a terrible trick on the other, to scare them, and was keeping the children hidden somewhere. They ordered Eddie and Alice Crimmins to put an end to this little game, *immediately*. Still, they began to prepare for the worst and considered all possibilities. After all, it was possible the children had slipped out through the window, as they had in the past.

If their careers in New York City had taught them anything, it was that madmen lurked around every corner. One hundred fifty police officers were dispatched to search for Eddie and Missy. From the sky, helicopters swept the area. On the ground, searchers scoured every basement and checked every bush in the neighborhood. The Crimminses' apartment was converted into operations headquarters. Neighbors came by offering their support. Women poured coffee; men helped with the search. Others kept their distance and stood in the street, hands on their hips, looking anxious or disapproving as they commented on the drama.

This had the hallmarks of a good scoop, and reporters soon gathered in throngs on the sidewalk. In their notebooks, they scribbled down the rumors and descriptions of sirens echoing through the neighborhood. Hours went by. Then, at 1:45 P.M., the phone rang in the Crimminses' living room.

Piering took the call.

After a brief conversation, the detective hung up and asked the children's mother to follow him. She put Brandy on a leash and, flanked by three investigators in suits and ties, walked out to an unmarked police car. No one told her where she was going.

2
Vacant Lots

Earlier that day, on July 14, 1965, nine-year-old Jay Silverman dared to disobey his parents. He ventured into an abandoned woodlot, which people in the neighborhood occasionally used as an illegal dumping ground. For Jay, playing in the vacant lot was strictly forbidden, as his parents worried he might hurt himself or pick up something dirty. But after a fight with his sister, an indignant Jay was less apt to follow rules. He pushed through the brush, drawn in by a curious swarm of flies buzzing over what he first thought was a broken doll. Before long, the boy ran back to his parents. They made the call to the Kew Gardens Hills police department.

When Alice and the detectives drove up to the scene, curious bystanders were hovering around the periphery, kept out by police tape. Detectives guided the children's mother through the brush. Though the grove was shaded and sheltered from direct sunlight, it held a remarkably heavy, suffocating heat. The path seemed to be laid out before them; all they had to do was follow the flies. In the distance, a small blonde, blue-eyed girl lay on her side, looking like a delicate broken doll. Alice took in the scene. She stopped ten feet away from the body, as the blood drained from her face and she collapsed. Piering caught her fall. When he asked if she recognized the body, Alice uttered only two words: "It's Missy."

Her daughter had been found less than half a mile from home. She was wearing her undershirt and underwear. Her pajama top had been tied around her neck and mouth, as if to gag her. Bruising on her neck suggested that the clothing had been used to strangle her to death. The rest of her body showed no signs of a struggle or blows. She had died without defending herself. Had she been sexually assaulted? Two details left detectives uncertain: A few hairs were found between her thighs and her anus was slightly dilated, though there were no lesions. According to investigators, there wasn't enough evidence to conclude that she had been molested.

As Alice Crimmins stepped out of the woods, still staggering and leaning on the detectives, she crossed paths with a second squad car. Her husband was the next person to be brought to the scene. Much later, in one of the very few interviews she would agree to give to the press, Alice revisited this exact moment with journalist Ken Gross. "I don't remember if they uncovered the body or if it just wasn't covered when I approached. [. . .] I don't remember if I saw her face. I don't remember if I passed out or not. [. . .] I don't remember if she was dressed or undressed . . . I don't remember anyone saying anything to me."

At the Crimminses' home, photographers were still hovering around the front entrance, waiting to pounce. This was their job. The story was sure to make headlines the next day, and their bosses were going to want the classic photo of the grieving mother to depict the tragedy. But when Alice Crimmins came home and their flashes lit up the neighborhood, the reporters couldn't help but be disappointed. Sure, there were tears running down her face, but the children's mother looked less distraught than expected. Piering took it all in. The first tears she had shed appeared to be for reporters. To Piering, this was a clue. And now it was time to collect more evidence.

The case had gone from an alarming disappearance to a homicide investigation—and a second child was still missing.

Three days later, on Saturday, July 17, 1965, on the day of Missy's funeral, the photographers were still hanging around. In an attempt to avoid reporters, the grieving parents chose the modest Church of St. Raymond in the Bronx, where Alice's father had been buried a few months earlier. Wishful thinking. When the Crimmins couple arrived, a mob of reporters and photographers were already crowding around the church, jockeying for the best shots. A flurry of shutters clicked as four men walked up the steps, lifting a tiny white casket with chilling ease. Behind them, Missy's mother leaned on her husband's arm, her face framed by a black veil. She followed the procession looking dazed, then knelt before the open casket and wept. Missy wore a white dress, and a white prayer book had been placed in her hands.

The scene left reporters unmoved, and after the ceremony, they began interviewing relatives of the family and spreading rumors. According to the police, the children's mother had reached out to one of her paramours during the service, suggesting they meet afterward. During the funeral, prayers were made to bring little Eddie home safely. The NYPD extended the search area to include all of Queens, and hundreds of people were interviewed. But they found no sign of the boy.

Then, on Monday, after days of search efforts, the police received the call they'd been dreading.

This time again, the news came from a child who had been out exploring. On July 19, ten-year-old Ralph Warnecke had been out walking with his father, Vernon, near Flushing Meadows Corona Park. It was a massive park in central Queens that was currently hosting the World's Fair. Millions of visitors flocked to the fair to take in the impressive, futuristic architecture and attractions, against a backdrop of Belgian waffles, beers, and novelties. No New Yorker was going to miss it. Alice's apartment was just a few miles away, and she had, in fact, promised to go there with her children for both their birthdays, in October.

This is where Ralph and Vernon Warnecke made their macabre discovery, in a vacant lot near one of the parking areas set up for the fair. An abandoned blanket and a pungent stench had caught their attention. As an Army veteran, Vernon Warnecke was all too familiar with this odor. Gingerly, he lifted the plaid blanket. What he saw was more horrifying than anything he could have imagined. He found a shapeless mass, blackened and barely recognizable. It was a child's torso, with the arms and neck missing. The body had been torn apart by rats and insects.

When police officers were dispatched to the scene, tailed by the perpetual horde of reporters, Ralph and Vernon were still there. In front of the cameras, little Ralph stood in his shorts and high socks, pointing a trembling finger at the bush where they had made the discovery. In the photo, he seems overwhelmed, his shoulders drawn up close to his head, looking like a child who has done something wrong.

This time, the Crimmins parents were spared the sight of the body. At the morgue, Alice Crimmins identified the pajamas she had put on her son the day before he went missing. She was given sedatives. The medical examiners took a while to formally identify the body, which was in a state of severe decomposition after five days of exposure to the summer heat and critters. They were unable to determine, with certainty, the cause of death. The body was examined by several members of the NYPD, including Dr. Michael Baden, who two weeks earlier had landed his first job as an assistant medical examiner. Despite his team's conclusion, Baden was of the opinion that all evidence suggested Eddie Jr. had died of strangulation, like his sister, and that both deaths occurred at about the same time. Both children had been found barefoot and lying on their sides.

Eddie Jr. was buried beside Missy, with little ceremony. This time, there were no throngs of reporters. The frantic search that had kept New York law enforcement and media on bated breath for five days had finally come to an end. The NYPD was now investigating a double homicide.

They began with routine inspections. Police spotted tire tracks close to the boy's body and searched nearby cars. But the investigation soon homed in on two prime suspects: the parents. Detectives had noticed inconsistencies in their accounts of the day leading up to the murders. The father said he had watched a movie on CBS after getting off the phone with his wife. But when a police officer confirmed this with the network, he discovered the film was not aired at the time indicated by Eddie Crimmins.

As for the mother's story, gas station attendants were certain she had not filled up the tank at 8:30 P.M., as she had stated in her first interrogation. They claimed she was there three hours earlier, at 5:30 P.M. One of the detectives pointed out that these kinds of mistakes happen when people are stressed and in shock. But when given the opportunity to change her statement, she declined and stubbornly stuck to her story, instead accusing the gas station attendants of lying. Another part of her testimony also intrigued the police: Alice Crimmins told them she had fed her children veal for dinner. But in Missy's stomach, the forensic experts had not found meat, but rather pasta. "In this case, the stomach content was extremely important," says Dr. Michael Baden nearly sixty years later.

At eighty-eight years old, Dr. Baden is a controversial figure, the kind of star that could only exist in the United States, a country obsessed with true crime. For thirteen years, he hosted his own HBO show, *Autopsy*, in which he literally dissected the country's history while investigating the deaths of figures like John Fitzgerald Kennedy and Martin Luther King. Most recently, the families of George Floyd and Eric Garner, two black men who died as a result of police violence, hired Dr. Baden to act as an independent forensic pathologist.

Now eighty-eight years old, Baden still remembers the Crimmins case. "When we opened the stomach, it contained a lot of undigested food, including macaroni or Italian food, which meant the little girl had died within two hours of eating."

   With this new information in mind, the investigators assigned to the case began to ask themselves more questions. Could Alice Crimmins really have fed her children at 7:30 P.M. and then seen them alive at midnight, as she had told them? Was she lying about dinner? And if she lied about that, what else could she be lying about?

3

"A Sick Mind"

One evening in August 1965, three weeks after the children's death, a convertible glided through the streets of Kew Gardens Hills. The car made its way through New York and crossed the East River over one of the bridges connecting Queens to the Bronx. At the wheel, a woman nervously checked her rearview mirror to see if she was being tailed by law enforcement or reporters. The driver was Alice Crimmins. Since the tragedy, she had begun going for night drives, with no destination or purpose. But on that evening, she had a very specific intention. She was heading for the Capri, an outdated bar in the Bronx.

In his 1975 book *The Alice Crimmins Case*, journalist Ken Gross describes the bar as "a place that seemed to belong to another time—a time of Italian crooners singing 'Isle of Capri,' of ambitious secretaries with rhinestone rings ordering creme de menthe, of double-parked Lincoln Continentals."

Why had she gone there? To see one man, a regular named Anthony Grace. He was a millionaire, married with kids, and twice Alice's age. At fifty-four, Grace was a small and thick man, with a hoarse voice and a pencil-thin mustache. Flecks of gray had begun to show in his dark hair. He was a regular at the Capri because his mother lived across the street. The man had come from nothing and built an empire, and now oversaw the construction of highways and parks across the state. He flaunted his success, driving shiny cars, wearing fine silk suits and waving around a ring that featured an impressive pink diamond. Alice and Anthony had met one year before, at a Queens bar called El Capitan. They had been dating ever since.

Alice spotted Grace's car in the parking lot. From a phone booth across the street, she called the Capri and asked to speak with a man she called "Tony." The waiter told her Tony had stepped out. He was lying, of course. She could see Tony's car. But it was a predictable lie. Since the death of her children, Anthony Grace had cut ties with Alice and refused to see or speak to her.

Was he afraid that their relationship would tarnish his lucky star?

In any event, investigators had still paid a visit to Anthony Grace. He was the person she had called on the evening of July 13, when she asked to join him at a bar, at the Capri. At the time, he had told her he was alone and that he'd soon be heading home. But this, too, was a lie, as investigators would discover. Grace had, in fact, been in the company of a few women he called "the bowling girls." In 1960s New York, this was a popular hobby for wives. The truth was some women never did make it to the alleys. For them, bowling was a convenient cover, allowing them to enjoy an evening out—often with other men—and away from their husbands with their suspicions.

During his first interrogation, Grace told police that he'd stayed in the Bronx that night. Later, he admitted he'd in fact gone to dinner with the girls at a restaurant in Queens, a few miles from Alice's home. "But why lie?" asked one of the detectives. To protect what was left of his marriage. His wife had regularly been committed to a psychiatric hospital, and he wanted to protect her mental well-being by avoiding public ties to the Crimmins case.

So he had lied about his whereabouts on July 13, first to Alice and then to the police. The detectives also came to realize that Grace was her gateway into New York's high society. But any investigation into Grace seemed to meet a quick end. He was a self-made man who could rely on his friendly relations with local politicians and the support of people involved with the Mafia, which at the time was ubiquitous in New York City's public works. He was sure to know men who could make or break a detective's career with a mere phone call. All investigators tacitly and unanimously agreed: It was best not to bother Anthony Grace.

Especially because a second man had already piqued their interest. Joseph Rorech had also been romantically involved with Alice Crimmins, and she had spoken with him on the day of the murders. Rorech was the man living in Huntington and the person Alice's husband had spied on the day before the children vanished. In his late thirties, Rorech was married with children. He talked a good game. His smile, though a little strained, was as generous as the layer of *gomina* slathered over his wavy black hair. The man liked to brag and was shifty-eyed, as if he was constantly under threat.

Like Anthony Grace, he was a contractor and his company offered repairs and handiwork. Unlike Grace, however, Rorech was running a failing business. He was a big spender, and this had put him in the red.

His profile caught the attention of the police, and one of the detectives was certain he'd seen three bottles of prescription drugs in Rorech's name at Alice Crimmins's home, on the day of the disappearance. The next day, the bottles were gone.

On the evening of July 13, the second call to Alice's home had been made by Rorech. He wanted his sweetheart to meet him and his cousin at a bar. But for some time by then, Alice had gradually been replacing Rorech with Anthony Grace, in her heart and on her calendar. So she made up an excuse not to see him. The story could have ended there, except that during the interrogations, Joseph Rorech offered up some intriguing details. He claimed that when he called Alice back later that night, the phone went unanswered. How could she not have heard it? Had she been out? He admitted it was possible he had dialed the wrong number, as he'd had quite a few drinks that night. Twenty-two cocktails, to be precise. For the rest of the night, Rorech did have an alibi. At 3:30 A.M., he had checked into a motel, as he often did, under one of his many aliases. He was not alone in this room.

Anthony Grace and Joseph Rorech were Alice Crimmins's most regular lovers, but they were not her only ones. Detectives at the Crimmins home found a black address book listing the names of her lovers. With this piece of evidence in hand, they were free to dissect her sex life. The list included many men, business owners, contractors, restaurateurs—and the number of a Queens policeman, who admitted he'd had an affair with Alice. His colleagues opted to tear out the page on which his name appeared and keep him out of the investigation, even though he offered to help. This address book was a ticking time bomb that had the power to shatter marriages and reputations, from the quiet suburbs of Queens to stunning Manhattan neighborhoods. To the police, the book was as fascinating as it was disturbing.

Roughly ten detectives were involved in this investigation, and Gerard Piering was neither the most experienced nor the most senior. But he had been the first to arrive on the scene and soon developed an obsession with the case. A man in his thirties with a short crew cut, Piering was just tall enough to make it into the NYPD. His suits were a little roomy, and he seemed to float in them. According to his colleagues, he wasn't particularly friendly, but he was hardworking. He didn't speak to the press, was never in the spotlight, but preferred to work in the shadows, toiling with fervor.

Since day one, he had been mulling over this question: How could a Catholic woman, from a pious and respectable Bronx family, end up as a cocktail waitress who takes lovers and chooses to leave her husband? To Piering, this was as much a mystery as it was an indication of guilt. It gave him ample reason to dig into her life.

Alice Crimmins grew up in the Bronx, in a modest Irish family. She came of age under the suffocating weight of a strict religious education with which she developed a strained relationship. Alice felt shackled by the rules imposed by the church.

At her Catholic high school, she was a popular girl who loved beautiful clothes, parties, and all things that glittered. She balked at the required school uniform and ban on makeup. Being unable to hide her face, which was pitted with scars from severe acne that had plagued her teenage years, always made her feel vulnerable. Alice therefore started wearing makeup as soon as she was old enough. The process of putting on her face became a sacrosanct ritual. Every morning, she concealed her imperfections—and her feelings—under an impenetrable shield of foundation.

She inherited this emotional discretion from her father, Michael Burke, a proud and impetuous

Irishman. Of course, she also inherited his penchant for defiance. Arguments between father and daughter were thunderous; she stood up to him but was also deeply respectful of his opinions. And when it came to his daughter's dating life, Burke was convinced that no man was ever good enough for her. In fact, he once made this abundantly clear to one of Alice's boyfriends when he went after him with a knife.

But with Eddie Crimmins, Michael Burke dropped his guard. The boy was the son of a colleague at the power plant where he worked as a repairman and was a good Catholic. So, in 1958, Alice did what was expected of girls of her age. She listened to her father and married Eddie. She was nineteen years old, and this was a sure ticket to boredom.

At the age of twenty-one, after the birth of her first child, Eddie Jr., Alice Crimmins quit her job as a secretary to become a housewife. Her days began to resemble what Betty Friedan describes in *The Feminine Mystique*. Published in 1963, the book is now considered one of the catalysts for second-wave feminism in the United States. Friedan describes a general feeling of unease that seemed to permeate the lives of American housewives at the time. The author describes "a strange stirring, a sense of dissatisfaction, a yearning that women suffered in the middle of the twentieth century in the United States."

Try as they might, at the end of the Second World War, to sell these women on the American Way of Life and the dream of a perfectly happy household, this model had reached its limits. According to Friedan, there was something missing in the lives of American wives, who could "no longer ignore that voice within women that says: 'I want something more than my husband and my children and my home.'"

Alice Crimmins was not an avid reader. It is quite likely that at the time, she had never heard of Betty Friedan. But her inner voice whispered the same things to her: This life was not enough. She needed more and didn't see why she should deprive herself of it. And thus, to the dismay of her husband and neighbors, Alice Crimmins danced. Alice Crimmins drank whiskey. Alice Crimmins shared her bed with men.

And the more liberties Alice took, the more Eddie Crimmins's resentment grew.

After Missy's birth, Eddie found out that his wife was secretly using a diaphragm for contraception, which he deemed a betrayal of her Catholic faith. In early 1964, the couple was still living together when Eddie began to suspect his wife was unfaithful. One evening, he secretly tapped their phone, then pretended to leave for work. Next, he crept into the basement, where he listened in on his wife's conversations. His doubts were confirmed. Just after Eddie left, Alice received a phone call from a man who said her husband was gone and the coast was clear. She received the visitor once she'd put the children to bed. Eddie waited fifteen minutes before going back into the apartment, in the hopes that he would catch them in the act.

This was the start of some cheap vaudeville. Finding the door locked, Eddie quietly unlocked it with his keys and broke through the door guard, which he had tampered with so it would fail more easily. He walked into their bedroom to find his wife standing by the bed, naked. Her lover lay across the bed, also undressed.

Eddie Crimmins threw himself at the stranger, who escaped through the window, leaving behind his clothes. He chased after him, but the man got away. By the time Eddie circled back to the apartment, Alice had fled with her lover's clothes. He doubled back and watched his wife's lover drive by, followed by Alice in her own car. She didn't come home until much later that night and showed no remorse. Alice maintained that she had done nothing wrong and that, in any case, he had no proof.

For Eddie Crimmins, this was deeply humiliating. The coup de grâce came soon afterward, in February 1964, when Alice asked him to move out. He gathered up all his belongings except the equipment he had been using to listen in on her. Even after their separation, he continued to spy on his wife. He would stake out the front of her building and told Alice he'd hired "Puerto Ricans" to watch her. When she was out, he would sometimes break into the apartment to sift through her belongings, often returning to his observation post in the basement to spend hours listening in on Alice's lovemaking. In these sordid moments, Eddie Crimmins was looking to hurt himself and collect evidence of his wife's infidelities.

In the year and a half spent spying on his wife, had Eddie come across her address book? The one the police found in 1965 was bound in elegant leather, the cover emblazoned with Anthony Grace's name, probably a corporate gift. Did Eddie Crimmins know about the wealthy contractor? Did he know how much he meant to his wife? Few appointments were written in the book; only weekly meetings between Alice and Anthony, every Friday night. As though he were the only man in her life. Eddie was mentioned only once in the book, and the reference was implied: On June 17, 1965, Alice wrote herself a reminder about Father's Day. Since her own father was dead, this must have been about Eddie. Maybe she wanted to remind the children to make a card or gift for their father.

Coincidentally, Eddie officially filed for custody of the children just a few days later. But he had been building a case for months, a process he had initiated after an episode involving Anthony Grace.

On Friday, January 29, 1965, in the early afternoon, Alice and her friend Margie had met up with several men, including Anthony Grace, on a yacht docked at a Manhattan pier on the banks of the Hudson River. The sky was gray and cloudy, the air was a biting twenty-five degrees Fahrenheit. The party was meant to last only a few hours, just enough time to sip champagne and say goodbye, but the men decided to treat themselves to a beautiful Caribbean escape. Alice and her friend hadn't planned to go along for the cruise. In fact, Alice had to get back to her children, who were with their maid, Evelyn.

But after a few drinks, the atmosphere changed. The men played a prank on the young women, locking them in the bathroom. By the time they managed to get out, the boat had set sail for Nassau, in the Bahamas. Or at least this is what Alice Crimmins told her family when she came back. Evelyn, the maid who had stayed with the little ones and who, six months later, would claim the mother owed her $600, told a different story. She said that Alice Crimmins had planned the whole thing and told Evelyn that if she was too drunk, she wouldn't be back that night.

One day went by without news of Alice, then two. On the Sunday, Evelyn called Eddie Crimmins to warn him and quit. She painted a damning portrait of the children's mother; according to her, Alice Crimmins often didn't come home at night if she'd had too much to drink. Apparently, Alice had even called in sick to work twice when, in fact, she was still drunk from the previous night's excesses. After the panicked call from Evelyn, Eddie Crimmins picked up his children on the way to his night shift and dropped them off with his mother-in-law.

On Monday, he finally heard from his wife. She was at the airport and asked if he could pick her up. After three days spent sailing offshore, the yacht had reached a port and she'd flown home as soon as she could. Anthony Grace had paid for the ticket. For Eddie, this humiliation was one too many, and he filed for custody of the children. In his petition, submitted at the end of June 1965, he formally criticized his wife in writing, alleging that:

- Item 6: "Immediately after the separation, my wife began to indulge herself openly and brazenly in sex as she had done furtively before the separation."
- Item 7: "My wife entertains, one at a time, a stream of men sharing herself and her bedroom until she and her paramour of the evening are completely spent. The following morning, the children awake to see a strange man in the house."
- Item 9: "My children are in serious danger of being irreparably damaged by the unwholesome environment in which they are living."

In this case, another person sided with Eddie Crimmins: Alice's own mother. She defended her son-in-law and claimed, on the record, that her grandchildren were the "innocent victims of a sick mind." Mrs. Burke had never accepted her daughter's separation from Eddie

Crimmins. A frail, pious Irish Catholic, it seemed inconceivable to her that a woman would disobey her husband or question the Bible. In May of 1965, when her husband died, she lashed out at Alice as they stood over his casket. She was convinced that Alice's indecent behavior had killed her husband. After the funeral, Alice Crimmins went to a Long Island motel, where she met up with three men and two women and drank heavily.

In the summer of 1965, in the weeks following the death of her children, Alice seemed to revert to old habits. She went out, often danced, and drank with abandon. In the neighborhood, everyone was aware of Alice's activities. A former student at a Catholic school in Queens recalls the atmosphere by the end of the summer, "There were three things I could always count on seeing in my Catholic school classroom: the American flag, a crucifix, and a statue of the Virgin Mary. Each of these fixtures served as amulets, protecting us against their profane counterparts: The flag stood against communism, the crucifix against Satan and, by the start of the school year in 1965, the Virgin Mary against Alice Crimmins."

4

Big Secrets, Small Lies

A small room lit by the glow of a single dim bulb. In the weeks following the children's deaths, Eddie Crimmins was forced to spend long hours in this gloomy box. Although most investigative efforts were focused on Alice, her husband was also subjected to several grueling interrogations. Eddie was a massive man with big hands and broad shoulders. Under the pale light, he answered the inspectors' questions. They hoped to make him crack, repeatedly asking Eddie how he had killed his children. They brought up the fact that he had ordered gin and tonics on the night of the murders, even though he rarely drank cocktails, as if he had wanted to be noticed by a bartender who could confirm his alibi. They pointed to his relentless surveillance of his wife. None of this made him look good.

In the investigation, new facts came to light. Most notable was a confession he'd made to his wife after their separation: He had allegedly exposed himself to little girls in a park. At the time, Alice hadn't taken Eddie seriously, as she suspected he'd made up the story to make her feel guilty for leaving him. But when investigators found out about this confession, Eddie didn't deny the allegation. He made up excuses, explaining that he'd done it to put pressure on her, that he was depressed. Inspectors asked if he had sought care to deal with his problem. No, none.

Still, Eddie Crimmins was cooperative throughout the investigation and never balked when questioned. He understood that this was a part of the process. His wife, on the other hand, was his polar opposite. She repeatedly accused the police of doing nothing to find the real culprit, and with every passing week, she became more reluctant to speak to them.

By August 2, 1965, she had become so uncooperative that Gerard Piering attempted an unprecedented approach. He summoned Alice Crimmins to a more neutral location outside the precinct. They met in a bar called the Tender Trap. The name could not better reflect

Alice's state of mind; she had become a nervous wreck, exhausted by weeks of surveillance and interrogations. Both parties talked over a few glasses of scotch.

According to Gerard Piering's subsequent account, when the conversation came around to the custody battle, Alice admitted that her husband would never have gotten the children anyway, that she never had any intention of ceding custody to Eddie. But what if the court had ordered her to do it? She would have taken them out of the country if she had to.

The detective tried to bluff. He told Alice he had evidence that the children had died two hours after their meal—although this is now the theory put forward by Dr. Michael Baden, it had not yet been formally established at the time of the investigation. If she had fed the kids at 7:30 P.M., as she claimed, then she could not have seen them alive at midnight. Perhaps she had gone out to meet a lover, left the children alone, and forgotten to lock the door? It wasn't too late; she could go back on her testimony.

The tension was palpable, with both Piering and Alice emanating a visceral animosity. He'd hoped she would see this as an opportunity to cooperate. Instead, she delivered an answer that matched the depth of their enmity, in a flat-out refusal to comply. "I don't care what scientific proof you have. In fact, you can take any scientific proof you claim to have and stick it wherever you want."

A month after the failed Tender Trap conversation, detectives shifted into a new gear. Both parents were asked to submit to a lie detector test, which would measure their pulse, blood pressure, and respiratory rate. Despite the fact that results would not be admissible in court, and even though the reliability of these tests had come into question shortly after they were introduced, the tool had become a staple in the 1960s New York police arsenal. So why not give it a try?

Eddie immediately agreed. His interrogation lasted two hours, during which he was asked a wide range of questions, from the mundane "What did you have for breakfast this morning?" to the crucial "Did you kill your children?" When he answered "no" to this last question, the machine detected no sign of a change in heart rate. In the eyes of the police, Eddie Crimmins had passed the test.

With Alice, it was a different story. Initially, she refused to take the test. She eventually gave in after four days of bitter negotiation, but on one condition: No one would be in the room with her or watching the interview, except the men running the interrogation. On September

1, she was taken to a small room at the police station and covered in sensors. They began asking her questions in quick succession. Then everything came to a halt. After about ten minutes, Alice suddenly tore off the wires and stormed out of the room. Nothing could convince her to come back. Especially not Detective John Kelly, who threatened to inject her with truth serum and warned, "While you're home [. . .] somebody climbs the wall and climbs in that window, kidnaps your two kids and maybe kills them there, climbs back out the window and carries the two bodies out. Is that the story we're supposed to believe? Most of us [never] believed it. If you're not guilty, this is your only chance to prove it, Alice."

What could explain the young mother's reaction? Two versions stand in stark opposition.

Alice claimed that once she was set up in the interrogation room, she heard muffled snickers and saw the glow of a cigarette behind a one-way mirror. She felt betrayed. Despite the agreement she had made with the detectives, several men were watching her answer the questions.

The investigators maintained that Alice Crimmins had walked out during the test because she was failing and the polygraph needles were "hopping up and down like a yo-yo."

❖

Sometimes an investigator's convictions can be based on the most minute detail. In the Crimmins case, detectives' beliefs were largely built upon this polygraph story. So far, both parents had presented inconsistencies that could point the investigation toward one or the other. After the lie detector incident, the police no longer had any real doubts.

Forget the disturbing story about Eddie's exhibitionism. Forget the hours he'd spent spying on his wife or the film he claimed to have watched on the night of the crime, even though it was not broadcast at that time. And forget the fact that after the discovery of the bodies, the children's father had asked very specific questions about their injuries, wanting to know the smallest and most sordid details, as if to gauge how much evidence investigators had gathered. Forget the fact that he had a spare set of keys to Alice's apartment and that his potential motive was crystal clear: revenge for the humiliations that his wife had made him endure. And forget that the day before his test, Eddie went to the library to read everything he could about polygraph tests, where he likely learned that by keeping his stress under control, he would be able to trick the machine.

In an act of collective amnesia, detectives seemed to forget it all. They had always believed that Eddie Crimmins wasn't smart enough to commit the crime, so his positive test result practically proved his innocence. They could now focus all their attention on the children's mother, the person they'd known was guilty from the start.

The press told the same story as law enforcement. Alice Crimmins had walked out of her lie detector test because she was failing, and thus was lying. Since the beginning, journalists and police officers had been communicating regularly. Every day, reporters could be found pacing in front of the precinct, hoping to glean information that would make headlines in the next day's paper. On the record, investigators remained tight-lipped, guarding what little they knew. But behind the scenes, they vented their frustration to journalists. One of the parents had to have done this. It was immoral for a woman to sleep with so many men. And an immoral mother could have killed her children, right? Newspapers were quick to twist the facts, exaggerating every detail of the story.

For instance, Alice Crimmins had worked as a secretary for most of her relatively short career before becoming a housewife and had only been a cocktail waitress for six months. Still, this last job was high-lighted in every article, along with descriptions of her appearance. She was referred to as "an attractive red haired ex-cocktail waitress" and "a shapely blonde." In the newspapers, Alice Crimmins came to be known as "the Queens housewife with hamster morals," "a Circe, an immoral woman." She fainted? No one cared. She had probably done it on purpose, to avoid having to explain herself. She didn't cry enough? The press took offense; a mother with dry eyes couldn't be entirely innocent.

Few journalists sided with her. One of the only reporters who questioned her guilt was Ken Gross, who worked for the *New York Post* at the time and managed to secure several lengthy interviews with Alice. Almost sixty years have gone by since the Crimmins murders. It has been years since he left his career as a reporter to become a writer. Gross has lived in Brooklyn for decades, a borough in which chess players once congregated and where hipsters now hurry to buy lattes from the area's myriad coffee shops. There's a school next to his building, and girls hang around the entrance wearing shirts that say things like "Little Feminist."

Times have changed, but Gross's opinions about the case have not. "Because I had empathy for Alice

Crimmins, everyone thought I had an affair with her," he explains. According to him, in trying to avoid the press, she lost the battle of public perception. In the eyes of the public, every subsequent silence further cemented her reputation as the stereotypical frigid mother who was indifferent to her children's fate. As Gross recalls, everyone admired the Kennedys in the 60s because they had kept their grief private. But in Alice Crimmins's case, it signaled her guilt instead. One day, in a Queens steakhouse, she had said to him, "I never got a chance to grieve for my children . . . I never got a chance to grieve. From the first, I was a suspect, and so I got angry. That became my grief."

He and many of the people who spoke with her in private describe a woman who was sweet, passionate, and spontaneous—quite the opposite of everything written about her. "Yes," he says, "Alice Crimmins did cry. But rarely in public." He admired her for that. "It's a very Irish Catholic thing. You're not gonna give up your emotions to strangers. Irish people shield themselves behind a lot of defenses. She was shielded and secretive, and she was brave." In those turbulent years, she wrote to Anthony. Ken Gross's impression of Alice Crimmins is confirmed in her letters, which are now available in the New York City Municipal Archives.

On paper, far from inquisitive reporters and suspicious detectives, she shared her agony as if confiding in a diary. She wrote with a steady hand, in a fine cursive. Even when she admitted to having a few glasses of scotch and feeling dead tired, knocked flat by the liquor, her penmanship was consistent, elegant. Page after page revealed a wounded and jealous woman who watched helplessly as her world collapsed a little more every day. "Everything seems to be shattering all around me, even my faith in people."

Though Anthony Grace had been ignoring her, she wrote to him, told him she wanted to see him again, told him about the TV she'd watch in a stupor every evening before falling asleep, about her upcoming horseback ride the next weekend, where she might pass through his property, at a bend in a country road. She wrote about her friends. About those who had pulled away from her, especially the other mothers. She wrote about the last of her faithful friends, Margie, with whom she'd gone on the disastrous cruise to the Bahamas. The two friends still went out together, and Margie was helping her plan for the future. Perhaps they would move in together and live as roommates, because Alice couldn't bear to live alone.

In the meantime, she was staying with her mother and had just picked up stenography again, to find a job as a secretary. She also wrote a few lines about the puppy Brandy had recently given birth to. "Her puppy is fantastic. It's so fat and ugly." She wrote about everything . . . except her children.

Then, at the end of the summer of 1965, cornered by police officers and journalists, Alice Crimmins made an unexpected decision. She packed up her things and left her mother's home to move into an apartment in Queens, where she lived not alone, not with a roommate, but with a man.

5

Surveillance

Only about five miles stood between Alice Crimmins's new apartment and the home she had shared with her children. She sought refuge in the north end of Queens, in the Beechhurst neighborhood, at the foot of the Throgs Neck Bridge that spanned the East River, in the Le Havre development—a collection of thirty identical eight-story buildings. From here, Alice could see the Bronx, her hometown, where her two children were buried. Anthony Grace's favorite restaurant was on the ground floor.

She had hoped to put enough distance between herself and Kew Gardens Hills to escape the gossip, after making the front page of the tabloids all summer long. But it was in vain. Everyone there knew who she was, and few people spoke to her. While no name was listed on her intercom, Alice's neighbors all knew who that man was, the man who shared her apartment. It was Eddie Crimmins.

In a letter from early August 1965, Alice told Anthony Grace that her lawyer was recommending she "put on an act" to get back together with her husband, to save appearances. She vehemently rejected the idea.

"I can't and that's all that's to it. I'm not being entirely selfish in my motives. Everyone around me has been hurt enough. I think of what would happen and the hurt it would cause when after a month I "dropped the act." There are people who agree with me, and one of them is my husband. I don't care that Mike* says that would be good for public appearances."

And yet just a few weeks later, there they were, playing the game. Husband and wife seemed to have patched things up and were even trying to establish a semblance of normal life. Eddie went back to work at the airport. Alice got a job as a secretary. They finally settled back into a routine—extramarital adventures included.

Before the Crimminses moved in, detectives carried out a secret mission in their new home. They bugged

_____

* Her lawyer, Michael Lo Penna.

the apartment, installing microphones in the kitchen and bedroom walls, eventually tapping the phone. They set up an observation post in a hospital room across the street. For twenty hours a day, seven days a week, a dozen policemen took turns scrutinizing the most mundane details of Alice's life. All of them men. And, as was the norm in New York, most of the police force was of Irish descent. Like Gerard Piering, they were Catholic fathers who saw Alice Crimmins's swinging lifestyle as much more than an alternative way of life. It was an insult to all that had shaped their beliefs.

By spying on Alice Crimmins, they discovered a world of parties, debauchery, and deceit, a world in which single mothers raised their children on welfare and indulged in the joys of nightlife, with *several* lovers. They saw a world in which wives lied to their husbands. To add insult to injury, this world reeked of Manhattan. In their beloved Queens, a neighborhood that was typically home to taxi drivers, housekeepers, small contractors, and policemen—people who kept the city running every day—everything was a little more drab, more modest, and smaller than out there in The City. In Queens, rock bands often played subdued covers, while patrons nursed glasses of cheap scotch. In the audience, you could find simple insurance brokers or lawyers with little ambition. They were there to dance to songs by the Beatles and the Beach Boys or to the Rolling Stones' "(I Can't Get No) Satisfaction." After dark, they would roam the streets, looking for a little thrill. Sitting in imitation leather chairs, for the length of one song or a night, they might forget their wives.

Of course, throughout their careers, the detectives had witnessed countless events that disgusted them. They couldn't ignore the fact that America was experiencing a cultural upheaval in the mid-1960s. But these changes seemed to be affecting places far from Queens, places like Vietnam and Dallas, and California campuses. Maybe even Harlem or the Bronx. But this was different. The crime had been committed just a few blocks from their homes. And Alice Crimmins, this recalcitrant woman who refused to obey them or speak to them, this "stone" as they'd taken to calling her, she embodied all that threatened their peaceful little lives. They were indignant. Even her children's deaths did nothing to curb her wild impulses. She continued to flirt and cheat on her husband, right under his nose, and in front of their microphones. One of the police officers figured Eddie Crimmins had to be either a saint or the dumbest man on Earth.

As the detectives spent caffeine-fueled, sleepless nights monitoring their recording equipment, they ruminated. Their hatred of Alice Crimmins festered and became an engine. Some even went so far as to say that if "the bitch" was their wife, they would kill her. Gerard Piering was both the youngest and most relentless member of the team. On his days off, he organized stakeouts, tailing his suspect's acquaintances as soon as he could. It became so frequent that people grew accustomed to his presence and would greet him when they crossed paths.

On the other end of the microphones, Alice soon realized that the NYPD was listening in. She knew her phone was being tapped. Then she noticed that some of her relatives, including her own mother, had agreed to wear a microphone when seeing her and that the police were wearing them too. Sometimes, when she picked up the receiver, Alice would greet the detectives with a "Hey, boys, drop dead!"

She perfected the art of losing a police detail. In the past, they'd only needed one car to tail her. Now, Alice knew how to spot them and would suddenly change directions at the last second. To keep tailing her, the police had to start setting up multiple vehicles along the road. This game of cat and mouse went on in a vicious circle; every time Alice fled, detectives became even more convinced that she had something to hide. And the more they followed her, the more she thwarted their efforts. The surveillance was unrelenting.

When detectives learned that Alice's new employer had unwittingly recruited her under her maiden name, they dropped by her workplace and exposed her true identity. She was fired on the spot. This occurred several times. When Alice eventually found a boss who was not put off by her reputation or by law enforcement, she began to have a relationship with him and immediately suffered the consequences, when detectives made sure to notify the man's wife. And on it went. Until one day, they came across something juicier.

Manhattan's Club 82 was a notorious establishment. Managed by the Mafia, the club would put on shows that were unusual for that era, even in a city like New York. Club 82 put on drag shows. Investigators found out that Joseph Rorech, the man who had called Alice on the night of the crime and invited her to join him, was a regular there. He was friends with the club's star, Hans Crystal, and was having an affair with a cross-dressing man.

Rorech was a shady character with crippling debt, a small-time crook and the self-proclaimed "best scammer in the world." He regularly used pseudonyms to sign counterfeit checks or book rooms in motels with women—*and men*. Investigators knew what this meant. Rorech was a man who could be pressured, especially since, unlike Anthony Grace, he had no ties to high-ranking politicians. It wasn't long before the police started blackmailing him. Joseph would have to choose between being a mole in the investigation into Alice or having his double life exposed to his wife. He took the deal. But he also warned the detectives that Alice had distanced herself from him since the children's death and had not shared her new number. Of course, this proved to be of little consequence, as the investigators made sure to give Rorech her number.

Rorech quickly got to work. He reached out to Alice, who invited him into her home. Soon, the former lovers shared her bed once again, recorded by an indiscreet team of investigators. The detectives wasted no time and informed Eddie Crimmins of the situation while he was at work. Eddie immediately called Alice. When Rorech tried to flee, he found that the police had slashed his tires in the hopes of causing an altercation between him and Eddie and to see their suspect caught red-handed. At the last minute, Detective Phil Brady stepped in to help Rorech escape and called a tow truck.

Brady was the only cop on the team who had any doubts as to Alice Crimmins's guilt. In fact, he was more suspicious of her husband Eddie, and even wrote a report to this effect, which he shared with his superiors. But they did nothing about it and—worse—Phil Brady was gradually excluded from the investigation.

From surveillance and tailing to dirty tricks, the detectives threw everything they had into this investigation. But as they patiently toiled to build the case, a few crucial questions remained unanswered. Not to mention the fact that certain procedural steps were botched. For instance, nobody had taken a picture of the window on the day of the crime. Gerard Piering maintained that when he first walked around the children's room, he found a layer of dust on the furniture beneath the window. According to him, this proved that no one could have entered through the window; otherwise the dust would have been disturbed. But again, there was no photo evidence to support his claim. A few shots of the bureau had been taken, but only after technicians had covered the surface in fingerprint powder. Some physical evidence had also been lost, like the blanket found wrapped around little Missy's body.

In their relentless pursuit, were they hoping to compensate for these shortcomings? Were they blinded by their hatred of the victims' mother? For whatever reason, the detectives focused on this single theory and compulsively compiled details about Alice Crimmins's sexual life, recorded on hundreds of audiotapes. According to one of the detectives, the recordings were "sensationally concupiscent," and there were so many of them that journalist Ken Gross once surmised that the NYPD tapped Alice Crimmins's phone more than they did the Mafia.

Today, most of these tapes are inaccessible, and many have simply disappeared. Only a few remain, mostly recordings of her phone calls. For hours, listeners can hear the distant voices of Alice Crimmins and her lovers, regularly interrupted by clicking sounds and a low-quality connection.

"What did you say? I didn't hear you." The rest of the time, their conversations are just mundane day-to-day banalities.

"What did you eat?"

"What do you want to eat?"

"Lobster."

"What time are you going to bed?"

"I washed my hair."

"I shaved."

"I'm going to bed in fifteen minutes, how about you?"

"What did you do on Saturday?"

"Nothing."

"Fat Cat almost jumped into the washing machine!"

Tape recorders went on recording. The police tran-scribed it all. Tirelessly. For hours. Days. Months . . . twenty-six months, to be precise. During this time, they interviewed five thousand people. But they never found a shred of proof, no clues, not even a hint of a confession.

DELIVERING JUSTICE

6
Fear Over the City

A few miles from Kew Gardens Hills, another neighborhood bears a name so similar they are often confused: Kew Gardens. Once two parts of the same estate, the neighborhoods were separated by a railway and a thoroughfare built in the first half of the twentieth century.

A year and a half before the children's deaths, at 3:00 A.M. on a cold night in March of 1964, twenty-eight-year-old Kitty Genovese left the bar where she worked as a waitress and headed home to Kew Gardens. She parked her car just a short walk from her apartment. But she never made it home. A man stepped out of the dark and deserted street. He stabbed her, chased after her, and raped her. Kitty Genovese's attack lasted thirty minutes.

After the murder, the *New York Times* published a shocking article: Thirty-eight witnesses had heard the young woman's screams and calls for help, but not one person had called the police. This struck a nerve across the country. So now people could be brutally murdered in the streets of New York and the response would be utter indifference? Had the country's most famous city really become so devoid of humanity?

Over the years, further research would show that this story about the thirty-eight impassive witnesses was false, or at the very least a gross exaggeration. In 2016, the very same *New York Times* reexamined its investigation into the events and identified mistakes in their original reporting. Few neighbors had actually heard the screams. But in the collective memory, the legend lives on. A psychological theory was even named after the story. It's called the "Kitty Genovese effect" and suggests that when a person is crying out for help, the more witnesses there are, the less people will tend to react.

The crime also led authorities to develop the United States' first national emergency call center, the predecessor of today's emergency 911 number. To this day, the name Kitty Genovese evokes New York City's dark days in the 1960s, when crime and homicide rates were skyrocketing as the city descended into ever more violence against the backdrop of social, cultural, and economic unrest.

Just over a year after Kitty Genovese's death, the Crimmins children's murders sent a chill through Queens yet again. Until that point, the history of Kew Gardens Hills had been uneventful; now, residents were locking their doors. Deadbolts and door guards were double-checked; guns were loaded. The day after Missy's body was discovered, one of Alice Crimmins's neighbors told the press, "Everyone is on edge. I have four boys, and let me tell you, my gun is loaded and ready, in the corner of my room. I'm not taking any chances, and no man alive is getting near my children."

Residents were especially concerned because four days before Eddie and Missy's disappearance, a few blocks from Alice Crimmins's home, another event had sent the neighborhood into a panic. At dawn, a man had broken into the apartment of a Mr. and Mrs. Levins. The intruder woke up their four-year-old son, Robert Jr. and asked the child to come with him. But the boy did as he'd been taught and said he didn't have his mother's permission. So the man left without the child and snatched a wallet from the father's pants pocket. Neither parent heard a thing.

A few hours later, nearby, one Mrs. Davis saw the same man when he broke into her apartment on the ground floor and fled with her television set. The stolen item was found abandoned in the vicinity.

By patching together witness accounts, police were able to release a description of their suspect. They were looking for a man with dirty-blond hair, about five-foot-nine, weighing 155 pounds, age twenty-five to thirty-five. Distinguishing features included black-rimmed glasses and workwear.

Two weeks later, the NYPD was called again when a second incident was reported. A man had sneaked into a room in which two teenaged girls were sleeping, just across the street from the Crimminses' building. He did not look like the first suspect. The neighborhood was on high alert—not only had two children been murdered, but two different men were on the loose.

By the end of July, a delegation of fifty mothers and their children gathered to protest in front of the local precinct. They were demanding better protection from "prowlers, burglars, Peeping Toms, and other undesirable individuals." In response, the police promised to deploy additional resources. Every evening, starting at 8:00 P.M., two more squad cars would patrol the neighborhood, as well as two pedestrian officers.

This did nothing to quell the panic overtaking the community. Throughout the summer of 1965, Queens police switchboards were flooded with calls about suspicious individuals seen in the neighborhood. The media kicked into high gear. Newspapers all asked the same question. Could a prowler have killed the children? Detectives briefly investigated these leads. Exhibitionists and burglars were arrested and later released. The truth is, investigators remained convinced that a family member was responsible for the murders of the Crimmins children. "We don't believe these prowlers are linked to our case," they told journalists.

But their statements did little to slow the barrage of questions. If that was true, why had tragedy struck in these two neighborhoods where nothing ever happened? First Kitty Genovese, and now the Crimmins children? And Kitty Genovese's killer had been arrested after just a few days. So why was it taking so long to solve the Crimmins case? Journalist Ken Gross explains that under these conditions, Alice Crimmins was the ideal culprit. "In the collective psyche, if the children hadn't been killed by her, then it meant that everyone was in danger. But if it was her, then people were safe. It was so much easier to believe she did it."

Detectives desperately searched for evidence to back up this theory, but there was too little information to confirm their suspicions. They had no way to explain what happened on the night of July 1965, nor any details about the motive behind the double homicide. The truth was, they had nothing but questions. Why were Eddie Jr. and Missy strangled, and why were their bodies dumped onto two different vacant lots? Did the mother want to get rid of them so she'd be free to have fun and take lovers? But if this were true, and the children did bother her, why not hand over custody to the father, who had already asked for it?

Eddie Crimmins and babysitter Evelyn told the story of an unfit mother. On the other hand, many friends and relatives contradicted their testimonies, describing Alice as a sweet and loving mother. In fact, even her husband maintained that Alice could never have committed such a crime. So was Alice protecting one of her paramours? Had the children's deaths been an accident? For the police, so many puzzle pieces were still missing. Especially information that could officially connect Alice to the murders. And time was running out.

❖

In 1965 and 1966, New York was in turmoil. The city held two back-to-back election campaigns, one for mayor and then, one year later, another for the Queens district attorney. Both campaigns tapped into feelings of insecurity, verging on urban terror, that seemed to have gripped the entire city. On television, a new ad campaign was aired on repeat, asking the public, "It's ten P.M. Do you know where your children are?"

Queens District Attorney Nat Hentel was looking to renew his term. But to win, he would need results. And what better way to see results than to catch the killer in the Crimmins case? For hours, in tiny, closed rooms filled with thick, rising clouds of cigar smoke, his teams discussed the case with police officers and forensic pathologists to finally gather enough evidence to incriminate the children's mother.

Among these men was Hentel's assistant, Anthony Lombardino, a.k.a. "Tough Tony," who led the discussions with a particular ferocity. He spent his breaks sipping scotch in bars near the courthouse, where he told anyone who was willing to listen that if it came down to it, he would put the final nail in Alice Crimmins's coffin himself.

Late in 1966, just before the elections, Nat Hentel convened a grand jury. A panel of citizens was tasked with examining the evidence and deciding whether it was sufficient to hold a trial. They came back with a no, and Nat Hentel lost the election. Despite the setback, his successor, Thomas Mackell, continued in his footsteps. He, too, hoped to solve the case, and Tough Tony was still around to help.

The police brought out every piece of evidence they had and pored over the mail that had been sent to the precinct since the deaths of Missy and Eddie Jr. The stack was tall, containing thousands of letters, some anonymous. Some were mailed from a block away; others had been sent from across the country. A sorting process was in order.

First, there were the classics: people who were sure they'd seen Alice Crimmins somewhere, in a seedy part of New York or in transit at the Montreal airport. There were the psychics: people who'd had visions in which the killer's identity had been revealed to them, and they asked to be contacted as soon as possible. There were the enlightened types: people who felt that while Alice may have killed her children, her crime was still less grievous than those committed by women who got abortions. At least Missy and Eddie Jr. would be allowed into Heaven, unlike the missing fetuses. There were those who hoped to save the children's mother through prayer.

There was the former neighbor Alice had babysat for when she was a teenager and who simply could not "believe that the passion of Medea rests in that sweet, silly, vain little Irish girl." There were the women who suspected their own husbands; their spouses had been coming home from work later and later . . . perhaps they had a mistress and, by extension, might be involved in a double homicide?

And of course, there were those who had already condemned Alice. "She does not deserve to be called a mother, she is a threat to society, she deserves no mercy. Her naked body should be dumped into a city landfill, where rats can feed on her disgusting carcass." And "She is a vicious criminal, she will do the same thing again. Lax government invites lynching. We should make our streets safe. She is an alcoholic, a prostitute."

There was the disgruntled citizen who cut out a job offer and glued it onto stationery. "Bunny Type Barmaids—Over 21, attractive, and must have own costume," with the comment, "This is one reason we find girls murdered."

At last, among the thousands of missives, detectives found their epiphany, the one letter they'd desperately been seeking. Someone had seen something on the night of the crime.

The letter was written on November 30, 1966, a year and a half after the crime, and began with:

> *Dear Mr. Hentel:*
>
> *Have been reading about your bringing the Crimmins case to the grand jury and am glad to hear of it.*
>
> *May I please tell you of an incident that I witnessed. It may be connected and may not. But I will feel better telling it to you. This was on the night before the children went missing. [. . .]*
>
> *The night was very hot and I could not sleep. I went into the living room and was looking out the window getting some air. This was at 2 A.M. . . .*

What came next in the letter was a bombshell. The police decided to keep the revelation a secret. They would first need to identify the author of this anonymous letter and then convince them to come forward. When the mysterious witness finally agreed to testify, the prosecutor summoned a second grand jury—unsuccessfully—and then a third one, on September 11, 1967. That morning, Detective Piering nervously paced the hall outside the courtroom, complained that he had a headache, and got angry. The Crimmins case had become so important that careers were now on the line, his own included.

When the jurors announced their decision, Piering was exultant. After two years of investigations, Alice Crimmins had finally been indicted. She would only be tried for the murder of her daughter, as her son's body had been found in such a severe state of decomposition that the medical examiner's office could not determine the cause of death. Detectives would finally be able to arrest her and lock her up. They celebrated the news in a bar, where booze flowed late into the night.

By roughly 8:00 the next morning, Piering was ready. Truth be told, he had been ready for two years—two years of sleepless nights and sacrificed family weekends. He wouldn't have missed it for all the money in the world. With a colleague, he hid by Alice Crimmins's car. When their suspect got into her vehicle to drive to work, the two officers approached and informed her that she was under arrest. They told Alice she'd best avoid making a scene in front of the neighbors. She nervously gripped the wheel, before eventually giving in.

As they made their way to the police station, Piering turned to her and said, "It would have been easier if you had only told the truth from the beginning."

"Drop dead."

"It'll happen sooner or later."

"The sooner the better."

At the precinct, Alice Crimmins refused to have her photo taken, though it was required of all inmates. Head stubbornly bowed, she avoided the camera. But this was a fight she would not win. When she was eventually forced to lift her face and look into the lens, there was a glimmer of fear behind the fury in her eyes. Her lips trembled.

7

Bloodlust

They came at dawn and waited for hours. To kill time, they exchanged gossip and commented on the latest news. On Monday, May 13, 1968, the plaza in front of the Queens Supreme Courthouse looked like a bustling town square. The crowd was so dense that it spilled out beyond sidewalks and drivers struggled to make their way through the throng. Hundreds of curious onlookers were gathered, each hoping for a spot in the courtroom. These retired men and housewives had come from all over Queens and, according to the journalist Jimmy Breslin who was on location that day, "They came with chocolate bars in their pockets and pieces of ten-cent coffee cake wrapped in cellophane pouches in their handbags, and with blood-lust in their eyes."

The trial was to be held in the building's largest courtroom, but five hundred seats would not be enough to
accommodate everyone. When the doors finally opened,
the rat race began. Women shouted and clawed at each
other, clutching their handbags, while men, in dress
shirts without ties, elbowed their way through the crowd,
holding the day's newspaper rolled up under their arms.
Cigarettes, perfume, and sweat permeated the air.

To the journalists who were carefully recording the
public's resentment in their notepads, women wanted to
make it clear that they were mothers themselves. They
told them how many children they had, as if this gave
them special authority to weigh in on the case. About
Alice Crimmins, they exclaimed, "That bitch! That filthy
bitch! I don't understand it, I sacrificed everything for
my kids."

And finally, she arrived. With her face partially
hidden beneath a wide hat, Alice Crimmins was greeted
by a jeering crowd. She took her seat at the defendant's
table, stoic, back straight. She would go on to keep her
back to the public for the entire trial, never looking into
the eyes of the spectators who had packed into the courtroom benches and who stood out in the hall, paragons
of virtue and representatives of an outraged puritanical
America. Nor did she read the nation's motto displayed

on the back wall, the embodiment of a religious morality that weighed especially heavy in this case: "In God We Trust."

Alice Crimmins appeared before the court a free woman. Eight months had gone by since her arrest in September 1967. The police had wanted to keep her behind bars so they could crack her, but Judge Charles Margett had set the bail at $25,000—three times less than detectives would have liked—and her loved ones settled the payment on the night of her arrest. As soon as she left the courtroom, Alice went out for drinks with friends, as disheartened detectives stood by. They settled back into a familiar routine. Alice continued to maintain that she was innocent, while detectives waited for the day she would finally crack. The prosecution had a theory to present in court: Alice Crimmins killed her daughter, probably in a fit of rage and without premeditation. She then called someone to get rid of the body and make her son disappear, because he'd been a witness to his sister's murder. But prosecutors were prohibited from publicly mentioning the second part of the scenario. Since Alice was only on trial for the murder of her daughter, her son's death would be irrelevant in court. The outcome of this case was anybody's guess.

The jury was made up of twelve men. They were dressed for the occasion: a neat suit and tie, a matching hat for some, others with raincoats carefully folded over their forearms. Every outfit was purchased from a modest shop. Most of them could not afford luxury suits. They were machinists, electricians, small importers, and retirees. All were married and over the age of forty-five. In short, this panel represented the average Queens man. The few women asked to join the jury found an excuse not to participate, stating that they'd already made up their minds or that the defendant had to be guilty.

This was going to be one of New York's trials of the decade, and all media outlets were in attendance. Irene Cornell, a reporter for the local WCBS radio, was one of the few women present. She had made her way into the male-dominated world of journalism by covering trials without her boss's consent, eventually establishing herself as an essential point of contact in the field. "The spectators all had something to say," she recalls today. "They all had their opinions about Alice. And according to them, she was a murderer."

Alice Crimmins arrived with her husband, who was one of the first to speak. Between statements, Eddie Crimmins would look over at his wife and wink. He swore that his wife had not killed her children, and neither had he.

Next, it was Detective Gerard Piering's turn to speak. He was categorical. While searching the apartment on the day of the disappearance, he had found leftover manicotti, Italian pasta, in the refrigerator and an empty pasta package in the trash. This would support the theory that the mother might have lied about what she had made for supper. But there was a problem. The package had not been kept as evidence, and Detective Piering had failed to record this finding in his initial report. Perhaps he'd considered the information irrelevant at the time.

But this detail took on a completely different significance when forensic scientists discovered pasta in the little girl's stomach. There was no doubt about this point. Inside Missy's stomach, they had found carrots, potatoes, greens, fruits, chewing gum, and pasta, but no remnants of veal. Despite the accusation, Alice Crimmins consistently maintained that she had fed the children veal for dinner. Piering also focused on the layer of dust covering the bureau under the window. Again, he did so without any physical evidence to support his story.

Chief Medical Examiner Milton Helpern was next on the stand. In the factual and neutral tone of a forensic pathologist, he confirmed the most incriminating fact: Missy had died two hours after her last meal. Her mother therefore could not have seen her alive at midnight. This was one of the prosecution's most valuable pieces of evidence.

But what the jurors and the defense team could not have known was that the time of death had been the subject of lengthy discussions between detectives and forensic experts in the months following the double homicide. In fact, Helpern had initially placed the deaths between 10:00 P.M. and 4:00 A.M., and this range was only made shorter after several conversations with detectives. It was journalist Ken Gross who brought the information to light, and only years later. For the defense, Helpern's testimony came as a blow. And the prosecution had other cards up their sleeve.

Three days before the trial, Joseph Rorech disappeared. His wife said she had no idea where he might be. In reality, he was nearby, in a Long Island motel. This time, Alice Crimmins's lover was not with his latest conquest but with law enforcement. The police kept him there in isolation for several days, during which they made sure of two things: that Rorech would have no contact with the outside world and that the scotch would be bottomless. Since the last time he had seen Alice Crimmins, Rorech had fallen into debt again. Creditors were coming after him, the Nassau County police wanted him for fraud, and his accounts were so far into the red that he had sent his wife out to peddle encyclopedias door to door. To ensure his loyalty, NYPD detectives made a new offer that he simply could not refuse. Rorech would be granted immunity for all crimes he'd been accused of, except any cases of adultery or murder. In exchange, he would take the stand and testify.

On the seventh day of the trial, Rorech did as he was told. He was still a smooth talker, but his beguiling smile had lost some of its charm. With a slight tremble in his voice and twitching eyelids, he seemed on edge. After all, he was a cornered man. The prosecution questioned him about a night he'd spent in a motel room with Alice Crimmins, in September of 1966, a little over a year after the deaths of Missy and Eddie Jr. Rorech told the court that on that night, Alice had not been in her normal state and could not stop crying as she recalled the deaths of her children. He claimed that she told him, "There was no reason for them to be killed. It was senseless. The reason had been eliminated."

And that was when he asked her, "You mean, Evelyn?" She said, "Yes."

Evelyn was the maid claiming that Alice owed her money, the one who threatened to testify against her in the custody hearing. The prosecution did not ask for any further explanation. Joseph Rorech continued to recount their conversation.

He then asked, "Who killed the children?" to which she responded, "Missy and Eddie are dead. No one can speak for them, they will understand, it was for the best."

According to Rorech, after repeating this sentence several times like a mantra, Alice added, regarding little Missy: "Joseph, please forgive me, I killed her."

The courtroom was stunned—the defendant had allegedly confessed her crime to her lover. Furious, Alice Crimmins slammed her fists on the table and screamed at Rorech. "Joseph! How could you do this? This is not true! Joseph . . . you of all people! Oh my God!"

But Rorech was not done. He explained that Alice Crimmins did have a motive: She didn't want to let her husband have the children. In the previous days, she had even asked him for a list of countries to which she could flee with the children, where she would be safe from extradition. Rorech claimed that she stated, "I'd rather see them dead than with Eddie."

Two months after that infamous night at the motel when Alice allegedly made her confession, the NYPD had interrogated Rorech. At the time, he'd told them she was innocent. He had even reiterated this opinion just before the trial, when he testified before the grand jury. So why had he suddenly changed his story? He explained that his conscience got the best of him a few days earlier when his daughter celebrated her first communion. She and Missy were the same age.

Rorech and Alice locked eyes, as if they'd forgotten about the world around them. She glowered. He stuttered. Neither one seemed to hear the racket in the room: People were shrieking, crying out. Reporters leaped from their seats, ready to sprint over to a phone booth and tell their editors all about this sensational scoop. "What do you think this is, the Hippodrome?" Judge Peter Farrell shouted over the din. "I will not allow any more of this." He ordered the crowd to stay seated and stop talking. In the chaos, Alice Crimmins was whisked out of the courthouse, her knees shaking. Every man and woman in the courtroom stayed in their seat, lest they lose their spot.

❖

Since the beginning of the trial, another testimony had been highly anticipated, the one given by the "woman in the window." She was the person who had written the anonymous 1966 letter that convinced the last grand jury that a trial should be held. They waited with bated breath. A veil of mystery surrounded the witness, as prosecutors were keeping her identity a secret until the last minute. Every day, journalists interviewed as many spectators as they could, hoping to identify the anonymous witness. Perhaps she was one of them, sitting in the courtroom?

When the "woman in the window" finally appeared on the stand, Alice Crimmins did not recognize her. The witness, on the other hand, claimed to know who Alice was. Sophie Earomirski was a forty-three-year-old woman with round cheeks and a full figure. In 1965, she had been living on the same block as Alice Crimmins and her children, about two hundred yards from their apartment, on a cross street.

As hundreds of captivated spectators looked on, Sophie Earomirski took the oath and recounted what she had seen three years earlier at two o'clock in the morning, on the night of July 13 to 14. During a bout of insomnia, she had poured herself an iced tea and sat down by the window to get some fresh air and smoke a cigarette. A man and a woman came around the corner and walked up the street toward her home. On her shoulder, the woman carried what appeared to be a package wrapped in a blanket. A little boy walked by her side, his hand in hers. They had a dog with them.

At one point, the man told the woman to hurry, but she couldn't go any faster. "The dog's pregnant," she said, pointing to the animal. And then what? About halfway there, the man took the bundle from her. They headed for a car parked in front of Sophie Earomirski's window, across the street, and a passerby greeted the couple. When the man threw the mysterious package into the car, the woman anxiously exclaimed, "My God, don't do that to her!" to which he replied, "Now you're sorry? Does she know the difference?" The little boy climbed onto the back seat.

At this point, when Sophie Earomirski closed the window, the woman looked up at her and said, "Somebody's seen us." Sophie hid behind a curtain and heard them start the car.

The prosecutor asked her, "Now, the woman you say you saw [. . .] do you see that woman in this courtroom?"

Throughout her testimony, not once had Sophie Earomirski looked at Alice Crimmins. But in response to the prosecutor's question, she confidently pointed at Alice Crimmins, and the hammer came down. "It's her."

The audience cried out and Alice erupted, seething. "You liar!" she screamed. "You liar!" The judge called for another recess.

Why had Sophie Earomirski waited so long to notify the authorities? She thought the police could solve the investigation without her testimony, she said. Sophie Earomirski had been questioned roughly ten times during the neighborhood investigations and had told detectives that she had seen nothing; so why had she sent an anonymous letter two years later? She was afraid of being ridiculed, and her husband didn't want her to get involved. And most importantly, if she was so certain that she'd recognized Alice Crimmins that night, why had she written that what she saw "may be connected [to the case] and may not be."

The defense soon insisted that Sophie Earomirski could not be taken seriously. Proof—even people who knew her well didn't believe everything she said. She was known to exaggerate stories to make herself feel important. One year before the children's deaths, Sophie Earomirski had briefly worked at a kiosk at the World's Fair, where she had fallen and hit her head. Afterward, she swore, she had seen a "yellow mouse" climb up her arm, which had caused her to fall. One of the defense attorneys asked if she had undergone any tests at the hospital to check that her brain was functioning normally. With a touch of humor, she replied that her results were "perfect." The spectators applauded.

In the days following this second shocking testimony, the defense continued to try and pick apart Sophie Earomirski's story. She claimed that the woman she'd seen had bright red hair that fell below her shoulders. Several witnesses came forward to state that, in fact, Alice Crimmins's hair had been lighter and shorter at the time. And the comment about the pregnant dog? On the night of the crime, even Alice Crimmins had been unaware of this detail. The birth of the puppy a few days later had taken everyone by surprise. Other witnesses came forward to confirm this. It was a classic she said, she said.

One last person was now set to take the stand. And their testimony would end up devastating Alice Crimmins's public image. Or at least what little remained.

8
Alice vs. Alice

No one ever steps through the doors of Fillmore's Tavern by accident. This timeless Queens pub sits in the heart of a residential area, about one mile from Kew Gardens Hills. A single tinted window at the front protects those inside from prying eyes. In this room, people share stories about the present and their recollections of the past. The regular patrons keep the history of the place alive. Sitting shoulder to shoulder at the counter, they come together as soon as the pub opens, at eleven in the morning.

It's a spring day in 2022, and Jeffrey Abdale is the most talkative member of the group. From his childhood in the 1960s, he's held on to two significant memories. The first is the unforgettable World's Fair. At home, he's still got a box of memories from the event. The second is the trial of Alice Crimmins. As he recalls, he must have been between fourteen and sixteen, and a student at Archbishop Molloy High School, which was right next to the courthouse.

"We would skip class, sneak through the fence, and go to the courthouse," says Abdale. "It was the main event! We mostly went there for the air-conditioning and to see the very sexy defendant. Alice Crimmins always wore plunging necklines and short skirts. She wore provocative outfits in an attempt to wrap the jury around her little finger, but she didn't fool anyone."

Yet, in archival photos of the trial, Alice Crimmins is always modestly dressed. The only liberty she took, given the times, was to occasionally wear short dresses. Still, spectators and journalists alike were obsessed with her attire. Not a day went by without a news story commenting on her clothes. According to the press on May 24, the day Alice Crimmins was called to testify, she wore a black dress with long white sleeves and a matching collar. In her pocket, she also kept a large white handkerchief, which would prove quite useful because, again, she would end up in tears.

Her two lawyers, Harold Harrison and Martin Baron, advised her to testify. They hoped to challenge the media's depiction of her as a cold woman. It was a risky bet. On the stand, the prosecution would be free to ask any question they wanted and to scrutinize her sex life. And when the day came, they did not pull punches.

Assistant District Attorney Anthony Lombardino, who had promised to put the nail in Alice Crimmins's coffin himself, led the cross-examination. He had spent weeks preparing his questions and meticulously recorded every bit of information he had in a spiral notebook. His strategy was clear: to discredit Alice Crimmins in every aspect of her private life and give jurors the impression that she led a debauched existence. He wanted to prove that she was a bad mother and an unfaithful woman. After all, what kind of person locks her children in their room? And abandons them to go on an unplanned cruise?

He also compulsively listed all the names of her paramours and the points he wanted to emphasize, obsessively, asking, "What were you wearing when you were with this man? And with that one? What were you wearing in the pool? And what were you wearing in your boss's apartment?" Later, he told the jurors, "The presumption of innocence does not mean that the suspect is innocent," adding in the same breath, "The real culprit is here in the courtroom."

Within the first few minutes, the cross-examination had turned into a verbal jousting match that was anything but fair. Lombardino was a man with a booming voice, which he raised so frequently while addressing Alice Crimmins that the judge asked him to calm down. In comparison, her voice seemed to break at every answer. The judge ended up having a microphone installed so the audience could hear her. When she leaned over it to speak, Alice Crimmins seemed crushed. Questions and answers rained down like bullets.

"Have you ever cried in front of the police?"

"Yes."

"When?"

"You broke me down so many times it's ridiculous."

The public had already heard that Alice Crimmins had boyfriends. Some of her lovers were even called to testify: Anthony Grace, Joseph Rorech . . . . On the stand, Alice described her affair with Rorech. She claimed to have rejected him a few days before the trial, because she didn't want to see him anymore. Next, the prosecution dug into her relationships with seven other men.

In court, the audience learned that she had slept with her local barber—also her children's hairdresser—in the back of his car. That her husband had walked in on her while she was in bed with another man. That some of her boyfriends gave her an allowance: fifty dollars a week from Anthony Grace and a little less from Rorech. That she had gone on several cruises, like the one in the Bahamas and another to Atlantic City, where she attended the Democratic National Convention with Anthony Grace.

"And what about the pool at Joseph Rorech's home?" Lombardino pressed. "Did you ever go swimming in that pool?"

"Yes, I did."

"What were you wearing when you went swimming in that pool, Mrs. Crimmins?"

"One time, a bathing suit; one time, no bathing suit."

"Where were your children when you were swimming without a bathing suit in Joe Rorech's swimming pool?"

"They were dead."

A rapt audience reveled in every detail, alternating between giggles, whispers, and astonished shouts. In the next day's paper, a reporter commented that "the spectators got what they came for. For 10 days, they had been jamming the courtroom [. . .] waiting for the juicy testimony. Yesterday, they got the juicy stuff."

Ken Gross was there throughout the trial. He watched Alice's face crumple as she fell apart. "She failed to convey, to the people in the courtroom, the overwhelming loneliness she experienced in her marriage, the gradual numbness, and loss of respect." In an interview with him after the trial, Alice Crimmins revisited this painful day, when she faced off with Anthony Lombardino. "You know, going back over the transcripts—I mean, reading them—I know I sounded like a bitch. But that man started on me as soon as he got up. And I got angry. I just wanted to tell my side of the story, and all he was interested in was my sex life. I wanted to say I was innocent, but he never let me. He just kept hammering at the one point—my sex life."

In 1977, almost a decade later, the *Daily News* acknowledged that "the real subject is sex [. . .]. During the trials, witness after witness came to the stand with tales of the sex life of Alice Crimmins. If she had been dumpy or homely or middle-aged, none of this would have mattered. But Alice Crimmins was young. She was a redhead. She worked in a cocktail lounge. She was good-looking. And she had various affairs. The entire prosecution was conducted with a leer."

After thirteen days, forty-two testimonies, and more than 1,500 pages of transcripts, the trial was coming to an end. It was time for Alice's attorney to make his final argument, followed by Anthony Lombardino's closing statement. Lombardino hammered in one last deeply symbolic nail, in an attempt to leave an unforgettable impression with this final metaphor: "When Alice Crimmins testified on that stand, I couldn't help but think about . . . the one object in this world that has the most beautiful shape and symmetrical design—the egg. Just beautiful on the outside in shape and form. But when you break the egg open, if it should be rotten inside, it's probably the worst stench you can find any place in this world."

By the end of the trial, the forensic report was the only concrete evidence against her. The rest of the case relied on statements made by the State's key witnesses, Rorech and Earomirski. As far as journalist Irene Cornell was concerned, neither witness was credible. "Joseph Rorech was a truly sneaky guy. And Sophie Earomirski, who said she could make out the hair color? It was dark; how could she have caught so many details? The theory that Alice killed Missy and then asked someone to kill Eddie makes no sense. The little boy was known to be very protective of his sister. He would have yelled if she had been attacked in front of him. He would have fought. He wouldn't have obediently walked down the street with his sister's body." And especially not barefoot, as Alice Crimmins's supporters like to point out. Both bodies were found without shoes.

The jurors would have to make a decision based on this information. As they were escorted to have lunch outside the courthouse, onlookers shouted at them, "Convict the bitch!" A rumor had been going around; apparently, nine of them thought she was guilty, and three were unsure.

Meanwhile, Alice Crimmins waited across the street from the courthouse, at the Part One restaurant, which had been her HQ during the weeks of trial. By her side were her lawyers and a few relatives who had come to support her: her husband, her brother, and her mother, who was there for her despite their past differences. Alice ate almost nothing, draining one martini after another. The wait was unbearable, but when jurors asked to review certain pieces of evidence later in the evening, the pro-Crimmins ranks felt a slight sense of euphoria. Her lawyers assured her this was a good sign.

At approximately two in the morning, everyone was summoned back into the courtroom. Even the halls were at full capacity. Some spectators had used the recess to lie on the ground and take a short nap. It was late, but no one wanted to miss the long-awaited outcome.

When Alice Crimmins arrived, flashbulbs lit up the courthouse and the crowd gathered around, pushing her against a wall. Everyone wanted to catch a glimpse of the defendant. Overwhelmed, Alice Crimmins swooned, and the police had to surround her to keep the crowd away. She seemed a little groggy, perhaps from the stress—and alcohol. "The first thing I'm going to do when I get home is take a hot bath," she whispered to her lawyer's wife. The owner of Part One set champagne magnums in buckets and prepared a buffet. He was sure Alice Crimmins would be acquitted and back soon to celebrate the good news.

In the courtroom, Judge Peter Farrell was fed up with the circus ambiance that had prevailed throughout the trial. He issued a warning: If anyone made noise in the audience, they would be held in contempt. The room was dead quiet as the twelve members of the jury filed in. One of the men cleared his voice. "Your honor," he said. "We, the jury, find the defendant guilty of manslaughter in the first degree."

The judge's warnings had been in vain. Screams resonated throughout the room, and the loudest voice of all was Alice Crimmins. She collapsed, shaking, her body racked by deep sobs. Under a police escort, she was transferred to the hospital, where a doctor diagnosed a "severe state of hysteria" and administered powerful sedatives for two weeks. Upon hearing the verdict, Eddie Crimmins cried as well, and for the next two weeks, he went by the hospital every day in the hopes that he'd catch a glimpse of his wife through a window. He never did see her.

Eventually, Alice Crimmins was transferred to a correctional facility. She had been sentenced to a minimum of five years, after which she would be allowed to apply for parole for good behavior, and a maximum of twenty years.

9

Burn the Scarecrows

In theory, Alice Crimmins should not have been eligible for parole until 1973. But on September 5, 1968, after serving less than four months of her sentence, she was released from Bedford Hills Correctional Facility. Photographers immortalized her relieved expression, a face lit up with a broad smile that hid her tired eyes.

One of her lawyers had identified a breach in procedure that would allow them to have the verdict overturned. In the middle of the trial and in the middle of the night, three members of the jury had gone to Sophie Earomirski's address to determine whether she really could have seen what she claimed to have witnessed. But this kind of initiative was strictly prohibited, so the defense appealed the guilty verdict. As she waited for the

court to issue a ruling, Alice Crimmins was released
from prison and, again, bail was set at $25,000. In
1969, just a few months later, the Supreme Court of
New York ruled that the jurors' excursion had inter-
fered with the proper conduct of the trial. She would
have to be retried.

In the months following her release, Alice Crimmins
led a less flamboyant life than she had in the past. She
dyed her red hair a dull blonde and tried to be forgotten.
Her makeup became a form of camouflage, and now
when she applied blush and eyeshadow in the morning,
it was in an attempt to change her appearance. Yet try as
she might, she could never go unnoticed. Everyone knew
her name. In official documents, she stopped being Alice
Crimmins after she and Eddie finally divorced. Alice
moved back in with her mother in the Bronx, and took
up the name and habits of her youth. She became Alice
Burke again. But in the eyes of the world, she would
always be Alice Crimmins.

She was a free woman, yes, but something inside her
seemed to have died. She was no longer seen in bars, no
longer seen partying. Many of her friends turned their
backs on her. She became acquainted with solitude and
spent her days reading and going to the movies, where
she could hide from prying eyes. Alice grew closer to

her brother, who had become a pillar in her life since her children's deaths. She spent time with her nephews.

She began dating a man too, discreetly. It was Anthony Grace, the only one of her lovers who had stuck with her. Since the trial, his world had also been turned upside down when his wife, after learning of his double life, had filed for divorce. Later she'd been committed to a psychiatric hospital again, until her death in 1970. Anthony and Alice were both single now and free to begin seeing each other again. They took a few trips on his yacht.

It was as though her life was on pause as she awaited the second trial. In preparation, Alice Crimmins did as her brother recommended and changed lawyers, hiring two legal heavyweights: Herbert Lyon and William Erlbaum. The attorneys established a new strategy, in which Alice would speak to the press. Until this point, Alice Crimmins's story had been covered extensively but was often incomplete or distorted, only ever told by the NYPD and lawyers. The public had never heard from Alice herself. It was time for her to take the plunge and give her first major interview. For Lyon and Erlbaum, Ken Gross was the obvious choice.

He and Alice Crimmins had their first meeting in the spring of 1971, at a Long Island grill. He kept the questions coming as she steadily worked through scotch and cigarettes. She told him about her children. Eddie would have been ten years old in October 1969, and Missy would have been nine. "I keep seeing children that age on the street or somewhere and wondering what they would have looked like." Their smiles as four- and five-year-olds were forever frozen in a photo she kept tucked away in her wallet.

To another reporter, she said, "When I was a child, I had a recurring dream. I would dream that I was falling into a very deep hole, and in that dream, I would struggle to get back to the surface, toward the light. After the deaths of my children, my life was like that dream, except for one major difference. I wasn't trying to fight. Nothing mattered anymore."

With Ken Gross, she also shared stories about her daily life. The previous summer, she had discovered a new passion: baseball. Anthony Grace had a private box at Shea Stadium, and she spent time there "shouting herself hoarse" and cheering on the Mets, because she loved underdogs. She supported Muhammad Ali for the same reason. A month earlier, the boxing legend had lost to Joe Frazier at Madison Square Garden in The Fight of the Century. "They wanted to get him because of the way he talks," she said. "I saw a lot of myself in that. They wanted to get me too."

The time between the two trials would soon come to an end. In a few more weeks, Alice Burke would become Alice Crimmins again, at least in the press and in court. In a few more weeks, she would either be a free woman or condemned to another long prison sentence. "People expect me to prove that I'm innocent, but I can't prove it," she told Ken Gross. "All I can do is deny the accusations. [. . .] I can't think about anything, I just try to hold on, day after day."

The second trial began on March 15, 1971. Alice Crimmins was thirty-two years old. Gone were the round cheeks of her younger days. She looked sullen, hardened. And she wasn't the only one who had changed. Since her first trial in 1968, America had been rocked by social and cultural upheavals.

A few days after Alice Crimmins was released from prison, less than 200 miles from New York City, one event forever changed the course of history for women in the United States. On September 9, 1968, the Miss America pageant was held in Atlantic City, New Jersey.

Fifty candidates competed for the crown, all of them young, smiling—and white. The all-American beauty ideal heralded by the event organizers left no room for women of color. Not a single black woman had ever been selected to compete.

Protesters coordinated a response. Seven blocks away, the Ritz-Carlton hosted the first ever Miss Black America beauty pageant. For a decade, the civil rights movement had been spreading across the country and had now landed on the shores of Atlantic City, carrying another revolt in its wake: the women's liberation movement.

This was one of the first times that both battles converged in one location, in two parallel events. Organizers had chartered buses to bring hundreds of feminist protesters down from New York, and the women took over the iconic Atlantic City Boardwalk in front of the building hosting the official Miss America pageant. They criticized the event's racist process that "oppresses women in every area in which it purports to represent [them]" and set up the "Freedom Trash Can," a large drum into which they threw objects deemed symbols of their oppression: bras, high heels, wigs, curlers, but also *Playboy* magazines and mops. Some managed to sneak into the building, where they unfurled a banner reading "Women's Liberation" during the pageant.

It was all over the evening news. The concept of a feminist movement had made its way into the homes of American men . . . and women. Over the following months, the protests for women's rights multiplied. The second wave of feminism was sweeping across major American cities. Five years later, on January 22, 1973, abortion would be legalized throughout the country.

When he interviewed Alice Crimmins in 1971, Ken Gross asked her about the changes unfolding around her. She'd once told him that she liked to watch TV. From her living room, she must have witnessed the upheavals as they were happening: the Vietnam War, the fight for civil rights, the women's liberation movement . . . did she feel it related to her own life? "Oh, I'm for equal pay for equal work but not for all the far-out things. I don't hate men. I believe that women are put on this earth to serve men. A man should be dominant. I believe in women's liberation, but not at the price of my femininity." She added a personal story, "I had a bad habit when I worked in an office. I liked to take charge . . . I always had the feeling that I could do more. I wasn't cut out to be a housewife alone."

❖

While this statement can be interpreted as proof that in 1971, emancipation had not quite reached the quiet suburbs of Queens, the idea of gender equality had still begun to gain traction. In fact, divorce rates were seeing a slight increase. It was subtle, but something had changed in people's minds.

And from the very first days of the trial, that shift was evident. The crowd was thinner and less quick to anger than three years earlier. This time, the audience in the courtroom was smaller, the atmosphere more muted. The press seemed to have softened. The defendant's sex life made fewer headlines than in the past, and journalists spent a little more time questioning comments made by the prosecution. Some even expressed doubt, with one editorial piece stating, "This trial seems more like a story of revenge than justice."

This time, there were also more women among the reporters. A year earlier, employees at *Newsweek* magazine had filed a historic sexual discrimination suit. Confined to working as researchers, the women had demanded the right to work as reporters and to write articles for the magazine. Their lawsuit had a snowball effect, opening the door to similar claims in other media organizations across the nation. For the new prosecutors, the writing was on the wall: Clearly their old strategy, digging into the defendant's sex life to stir up fear and moral outrage, would no longer be as effective.

They were also aware that, under the US Constitution, a person could not be convicted of the same crime twice—a protection known as double jeopardy—and that Alice Crimmins would not receive a harsher sentence than the one handed down by the jury in the first trial, which had found her guilty of manslaughter in the first degree in the death of her daughter. They would have to find a different angle, something fresh. As fate would have it, the district attorney's team still had an ace up its sleeve. They had a witness who was willing to confirm that Alice Crimmins had confessed to killing her daughter and, in a major new development, to ordering her son's murder. In this second trial, the defendant was being charged with the murders of both her children.

The beginning of the second trial seemed to be a replay of the first, save two details. The defendant was facing one new charge and Assistant District Attorney Anthony Lombardino was replaced by Thomas Demakos, who found Alice Crimmins to be "an actress. A bad actress." The same witnesses were called to the stand, to repeat the same statements they had made three years earlier. Sophie Earomirski, who had caused a stir in the first trial, was all smiles as she posed for photographers. She was greeted like a celebrity by a row of beaming women who looked up at her with something resembling admiration. Like a triumphant boxer, Sophie Earomirski raised her fist in the air. But this time, when she spoke, the defense was not afraid.

Alice Crimmins's new attorneys had found out that three weeks before their client's arrest, the prosecution's key witness had attempted to commit suicide and was hospitalized for "nervousness." They cited a medical report in which Sophie was said to have suffered permanent brain damage. The defense was blindsided, however, by what came next.

Another former neighbor, Tina DeVita, came forward to corroborate Sophie's testimony. Five feet tall and barely visible over the edge of the witness box, she told the courtroom that on the night of July 13 to 14, 1965, she and her husband were driving home from a dinner when they saw "a man carrying a bundle, a woman, a dog, and a boy" in front of Alice Crimmins's building. This was the same as Sophie Earomirski's story. For the Crimmins team, the testimony was catastrophic.

The next morning, reporters were sipping coffee as they waited for the hearing to begin, when one of their colleagues ran in to share unexpected news. Alice Crimmins, who until this point had avoided them like the plague, was headed for the pressroom. A few minutes later, she stood before radio reporters' microphones, unsteady and with tears in her eyes, as she searched for the right words, and had to restart her sentences.

"I've come here to make an appeal [. . .] Anybody that lived in my neighborhood who might know something about what happened on the night of July thirteenth or the morning of July fourteenth. Anybody that saw something—or didn't see something. It doesn't make a difference either way because it's just as important to me [. . .] I'm asking for help from my side."

Journalist Irene Cornell inquired, "What prompted you to ask for help?"

Alice Crimmins swallowed, her voice breaking. "I need that help because I didn't kill my children. I swear I didn't kill them."

Later, her attorneys would insist she had taken this initiative without consulting them. Defendants were forbidden from giving interviews during their trial. The judge was lenient and issued a warning: If Alice Crimmins spoke to reporters again, her bail would be revoked and she would spend the rest of the trial in prison.

Her gamble paid off when the very next day, Marvin Weinstein, the head of a travel agency, took the stand. On the night of the disappearance, he had visited his

friend, Anthony King, who was living in the same
building development as Alice Crimmins. He was with
his wife, son, daughter, and their little dog—a miniature
poodle. At the time, he had been going to this colleague's
house twice a week. The whole family had left the prem-
ises at about two in the morning. His son was then three
and a half years old, and his daughter was two. When
the youngest would fall asleep, he and his wife would
sometimes wrap her in a blanket.

In the courtroom, Weinstein's wife sat in the audience, bearing a notable resemblance to Alice Crimmins.
Perhaps Sophie Earomirski had, in fact, seen Weinstein's
wife that night? The prosecutors were surprised that
he'd come forward so late. Why had he waited six years
to speak up? His response was that he'd said nothing
because he didn't think Earomirski's testimony would
carry so much weight.

Soon came another twist. The prosecutor found
a man named Anthony King, who contradicted his
friend Weinstein's allegations. He claimed that Weinstein was not at his home on the night of the crime
and that he had only ever come by once or twice—and
never with his poodle. A third witness, Sheldon Weiss,
was then called to testify. He worked with both of the
men and would settle the matter: King was a known

pathological liar. The defense had just scored one more point.

Throughout it all, Eddie Crimmins attended every minute of the trial, sitting right behind his ex-wife, next to his former mother-in-law and brother-in-law. But he seemed absent. When reporters questioned him, he appeared to have lost all conviction and spoke as if reciting a text he'd memorized. "I know Alice didn't do it. The police kept trying to make me say she did it; they kept trying to show me she did it. But I know her better than anyone. She couldn't do it."

On the stand, he looked even more discouraged. He defended Alice, but without hiding the fact that he now had little concern for her fate. "To be honest, I don't have feelings for her anymore. I don't feel sorry for her." With indifference, he added, "My feeling is that this matter has to be settled, one way or another." But there were more surprises to come.

10
The Mafia

In the second trial, Anthony Grace was again called to take the stand. In 1968, his testimony had been quick. This time, the examination went on for an hour and a half. Assistant District Attorney Thomas Demakos was more aggressive than his predecessor. Why had he cut off all contact with his mistress after the murders, ignoring her calls and letters for six months? Anthony Grace explained that he didn't want bad press. When Demakos pushed him, Grace stuttered. The prosecution's approach was aggressive, as if Grace were a suspect rather than a witness. At one point, defense attorney Herbert Lyon interrupted Demakos to ask, "Are you still trying to solve the crime?"

The assistant district attorney was, in fact, carrying out his team's plan. If the defendant had killed her daughter and then called for help to carry out her son's murder, as the prosecution believed, and if her neighbors had seen her in the street, then it meant a man had helped her. Nearly six years after the crime, this man had yet to be identified. But they could at least cast doubt in the minds of the jury, even indirectly. What if Anthony Grace was involved? After all, it was no secret that this man had contacts in high places, and in all kinds of circles, among shady characters. Some of them were even in the Mafia.

Once again, Joseph Rorech came forward to drop a bomb. Media coverage about his relationship with Alice Crimmins had cost him his business and marriage. And his worries seemed to be etched into his face. Since the last trial, his skin had become ruddier and creased with wrinkles that had not been there three years earlier. The star witness stood by his statement from the first trial: Alice had told him that she'd killed her daughter.

But now he weaved in new details that enhanced his initial testimony. He elaborated on the context in which he'd heard Alice Crimmins's confession in a motel on that evening in September 1966. He told the court he'd brought a newspaper that day. Splashed across the front page was a story about the arrests of thirteen mob bosses "bejeweled and carrying wallets packed with $100 bills." The article stated they had gathered for dinner at La Stella, an Italian restaurant in Forest Hills, when "detectives seized the underworld barons [. . .] and took them away in handcuffs, before Joseph T. Alcercio, owner of the restaurant [. . .] could present them with a bill."

According to Rorech, this had caught Alice Crimmins's eye. "I poured myself a drink, she sat down and read the headline," he stated from the witness stand. He went on, explaining that she suddenly started repeating one name over and over, then said, "I've never met this man, but I've heard his name many times."

The man was Michele Miranda. Known as "Big Mike" in his world, Miranda was one of the biggest gangsters in New York. He was known for his ties to Cosa Nostra and for having spent two years in prison after the famous Apalachin meeting, a summit of the American Mafia, held on November 14, 1957, that resulted in the country's first major takedown of mobsters by law enforcement.

Rorech claimed that in the privacy of the motel, he asked Alice if she had heard of Miranda through Tony Grace and that she answered, "yes." And that is how—in one, single sentence—Rorech drew a link between Anthony Grace and organized crime, at least in the minds of the jurors.

He claimed that Alice Crimmins continued reading and rereading the article, before starting to "sob hysterically." She then mentioned the murders and told Rorech, "The kids are angels. They're in Heaven. They'll understand." She kept talking and made that now famous confession about Missy: "I killed her." And about her son, she added, "I didn't want him killed. I agreed to it." In 1968, Rorech had not mentioned this second part of the confession in court. Perhaps it was because, at the time, the prosecution was prohibited from mentioning Eddie's death?

As he had done three years before, Joseph Rorech decimated Alice Crimmins without ever looking at her. As she had done three years before, Alice Crimmins seethed, glared at Rorech, and spat, "You miserable, lying worm." When he left the room for a short recess, she looked ready to hurl herself at him and shouted, "Why are you lying?"

Alice Crimmins's lawyers tried to poke holes in Rorech's arguments and accused him of making up this increasingly implausible story. The defense called Harold Harrison, Alice Crimmins's former attorney, to the stand. Before the first trial, he had also represented Rorech, who had suggested Alice Crimmins hire him as well. Harrison swore that when Rorech was his client, he'd never told him this or given any indication that Alice had confessed her crimes to him. Despite this fact, the prosecution had given Rorech a truth serum injection, hoping to get more out of him. And even under the influence of a powerful drug, he had never said a word about this story.

In all of Joseph Rorech's recounting of events, there were gaps and inconsistencies, including in his recollection of the night of the crime. Rorech had always presented two alibis: First, he was at a bar with his cousin, who corroborated this, and then he checked into a Holiday Inn on Long Island in the middle of the night, at exactly 3:34 A.M., as shown in the motel register. He was accompanied by a man who was never identified. He then left the motel at dawn and went straight home. But neither his wife nor his children could say exactly when he had come home that night.

Still, the prosecution continued to push the Mafia theory. One name came up consistently throughout the trial—Vincent Colabella. Known for his ties to the underworld, Colabella was serving a ten-year sentence for drug trafficking in Atlanta. A fellow inmate had recently told law enforcement that Colabella had confessed to being the driver on the night of the crime. Again, Joseph Rorech was there to corroborate the story. Although he had never mentioned Colabella at the first trial, he suddenly seemed to regain his memory and told the court that the name Alice Crimmins had given him was, in fact, Colabella. Rorech even claimed that Alice Crimmins had shown him a picture of the man.

The prosecution's story was beginning to take shape: After killing her daughter, Alice Crimmins had called Anthony Grace, who had sent her a henchman, Colabella, to take care of the dirty work, make Missy's body disappear and get rid of Eddie Jr., a problematic witness to the crime.

On April 14, 1971, the defense chose to call Colabella to the stand for the first time. He was removed from his cell in Atlanta for this occasion. At first glance, it did not seem to be in the defense's best interests to call him to the stand. It was a risky bet to bring a shady-looking prisoner—handcuffed and covered in scars—to a trial in which appearances had always mattered. But Colabella had information to disclose. First, he denied knowing both Anthony Grace and Alice Crimmins. No, he had not gone to her home on the night of the crime. In fact, he claimed he had never even set foot in Queens. And there was more. Colabella revealed that before the 1968 trial, prosecutors had come to see him in prison and implied that they could offer him a deal in exchange for his testimony at the trial.

If the prosecution had thought Vincent Colabella was the accomplice as early as 1968, why would they have waited for the second trial to present this lead? For Alice Crimmins's lawyers, it was proof that, from the outset, the prosecution's strategy had been unfounded and crude, preying on New Yorkers' fear of the Mafia. The second trial lasted one more week and ended with more questions than answers. This time around, Alice Crimmins would not take the stand. In his closing statement, Assistant District Attorney Thomas Demakos criticized her decision, stating, "She doesn't have the courage to stand up here and tell the world she killed her daughter."

❖

On Thursday, April 22, 1971, the twelve jurors began their deliberations. By the end of the day, no decision had been rendered and the judge issued the order that the defendant would spend the night in prison, pending the verdict. Despite protests from her family and lawyers,

Alice Crimmins was transferred to a detention facility. It took four court attendants to drag her out of her seat.

The following day, the owner of Part One restaurant once again pulled out the champagne magnums. He was as sure as he had been in 1968 that Alice Crimmins would come celebrate the verdict in his restaurant. Her lawyers were just as optimistic, although they refrained from sharing their feelings with their client. In truth, no one seemed to be buying the Mafia theory. Not the prosecutors, who appeared to have played the card as a last resort. Not the NYPD, who had never focused on this theory during the investigation. Not reporters, who never even bothered to dig into this lead.

That is why, at 5:30 P.M., on April 23, 1971, when the twelve jurors finally announced their verdict after seventeen hours of deliberation, the news came as a shock. Five years and nine months after the disappearance of her children, Alice Crimmins was once again found guilty of killing her daughter. And her son.

She collapsed. Her head hit the table as she shrieked, "Dear God, no! Please, dear God," and wept. "Sweet Jesus, not again!" Her brother shouted that she hadn't killed them. Eddie Crimmins, silent, cradled his head in his hands, wiped away a few tears. Even the reporters seemed stunned; Ken Gross was speechless, Irene

Cornell broke down and cried in a telephone booth. Rattled, Alice Crimmins's lawyer, William Erlbaum, commented, "I guess I convinced everyone but the jury."

So many questions remained unanswered. Why had the super's cart been under the children's window the morning after the crime? Why were the bodies dumped on two different vacant lots? If Eddie Jr. had walked outside in the middle of the night, why was his body found without shoes? Why was there pasta in little Missy's stomach? Did their mother lie about what she'd fed them, or could someone have fed Missy later, after her family dinner? Despite five years of investigation and two trials, no police officer and no prosecutor could answer these questions. And none of them could explain exactly when, where, how, and why Alice Crimmins's children were killed.

11
Women Make Movies

The reel from this film has long been kept in the back of a closet, like an embarrassing memory from teenage years. Even today, few people have seen the short film since it was made in 1971. For six minutes, it depicts amateur actors reenacting Alice Crimmins's trial in black and white, with all the excitement, exuberance, and clumsy passion of beginners. In a voiceover, a narrator says, "The evidence presented at her trials does not prove Alice Crimmins's guilt. Alice Crimmins was tried and convicted for a lifestyle that was unbecoming of a woman and mother."

The film, called *The Trials of Alice Crimmins*, was codirected by several women, each contributing to the best of their abilities and availability. They all met at feminist protests in the late 1960s, when New York was experiencing an artistic boom. In 1969, they decided to work together to encourage women in the film industry to emancipate themselves. And thus, Women Make Movies was born. Their goal was to bring a feminist perspective to a male-dominated field. They would do this by creating films directed by women and about women.

The Alice Crimmins case quite naturally ended up drawing their attention and became one of their first projects. Today, Ariel Dougherty is one of the few people who still has a copy of the short film. She is the cofounder of WMM and participated in bringing *The Trials of Alice Crimmins* to life. During the first trial, in 1968, New York's feminist movement was in its infancy. Activists like them only fully grasped the issues it presented once the second trial came about. "The media coverage [. . .] was bugging our feminist consciousness. Alice Crimmins was a controversial figure, and we did not try to say whether she was guilty or innocent. But I think our point, more than anything, is about media sensationalism and exploitation of women, and she's a classic example of that problem."

To raise public awareness about the issue, the directors chose to show the film to those who were first and most closely involved in the case: Alice Crimmins's neighbors, who had expressed such scorn for her. In 1971, the group of women bought a projector and a five-by-six-foot freestanding screen, which they set up for impromptu screenings in the streets of Queens. "We took it out into the streets [. . .] in the evening. [The film] was short enough that people stayed and watched most of it." But the operation didn't quite have the intended outcome. Of all the feedback they heard from neighbors, the one that most affected Ariel Dougherty may seem trivial. "It's good, [. . .] you're keeping people busy and otherwise we would have a lot of robberies." This feminist spotlight on the case also failed to make its way to the ears and eyes of reporters.

But Women Make Movies isn't the only group that attempted to have an impact. Just before the second trial, the New York Radical Feminists reportedly offered to help pay Alice Crimmins's legal fees. Her lawyers never corroborated this story. At the time, Gross interviewed one of them, William Erlbaum, about the connection between the Crimmins case and feminist uprisings. "No one has ever seen Alice Crimmins as a martyr of the Women's Liberation," he replied, before conceding, smiling, "but there is a bit of that." Four years later, in 1975, Ken Gross published his book about the investigation. He is certain that if the trial had taken place just a few years later, the outcome could have been different. "It was all a set-up. Alice Crimmins was the victim of a witch hunt," he says. He is still bitter to this day. "Women were just beginning to find out how oppressed they are or were [. . .] The trial goes to the core of the matter: what a mother's role is [. . .]. Don't put hooks on a door. Watch the kids. Protect the kids. Don't get laid. This was a bigger feminist issue than anything."

During the second trial, some "Alice Crimmins is innocent" graffiti was painted in the streets of Greenwich Village. But it soon disappeared under new coats of spray paint, new grievances, while the members of Women Make Movies moved on and started new projects. After 1971, *The Trials of Alice Crimmins* was never screened again. Over the years, the members of WMM developed conflicting perspectives on the film. Some started to feel it was too bad to be shown. Others wondered if, in making this film, they had, in fact, supported a child murderer. Alice Crimmins's ambiguous personality and the gray areas in her story have always left room for doubt. Even in the minds of those who are on her side, a nagging question sometimes rattles their faith. "But what if it was her?"

12

Bedford Hills

An hour's drive from New York City, Bedford Hills Correctional Facility is the state's only high-security prison for women. The original building dates back to 1901 and features an elegant red-brick facade and a stepped gable that are reminiscent of Northern European Gothic architecture. Heavy, gray, solid concrete structures were later added on. The eclectic complex is surrounded by barbed wire and guarded by an imposing watchtower.

Today, nearly 1,000 women are serving their sentences in this prison. There were half as many inmates in the early 1970s. Over the years, these cells have held notorious criminals like Kathy Boudin, a radical, militant leftist known for a 1981 Brink's van robbery in which a security guard and two policemen were killed. More recently, the prison held Anna Sorokin, better known by her con name Anna Delvey, whose story inspired the Netflix series *Inventing Anna*.

Life in Bedford Hills has always followed the rhythm of the nation's upheavals, some occurring in faraway places, others within the facility itself. In September of 1971, at the other end of New York, the Attica Prison revolt caused a national trauma. Prisoners had been demanding better living conditions and a riot ensued. When the uprising was eventually quashed, it ended in a bloodbath.

Three years later, in August of 1974, Bedford Hills experienced its own clashes; Attica now had a female counterpart. On this date, a group of two hundred inmates demanded proof of life from another prisoner who had been dragged out of her cell by several guards, and for hours, they took control of a prison sector. Less violent than the Attica uprising, the incident was barely mentioned in the press and has fallen into oblivion. Yet it had major consequences on the rights of incarcerated people.

In the wake of the riot, the women who led the revolt paid a hefty price for their insubordination. Eight of them were sent to a psychiatric hospital for men.

Without any privacy, they showered in front of patients, doctors, and guards—all male—and lived in constant fear of being raped by other inmates. They were forced to take heavy doses of neuroleptics, drugs normally administered to patients experiencing psychosis. In 1975, the women filed a joint lawsuit and won their case against the correctional facility. This legal action, in turn, led to more constitutional guarantees for women placed in solitary confinement.

In the early 1970s, another famous convict landed in Bedford Hills. ID: 71G0009. Name: Alice Crimmins. In theory, she should have been behind bars in 1974, at the time of the riot. Three years earlier, she had been sentenced to a minimum of five years for Missy's murder, as well as life in prison for Eddie's murder.

But the revolving door kept on spinning, and in May of 1973, two years after her second trial, she found out over the prison radio that the verdict had been overturned. The court yet again concluded that the prosecution had made mistakes. For instance, they should never have administered a truth serum to Joseph Rorech. And the assistant district attorney should not have said that the defendant didn't have the courage to confess to the murder of her children when she refused to take the stand. She would have to be retried and would therefore be released on bail.

She spent the next two years in limbo, waiting for the legal system and its endless appeals processes to issue a final ruling and seal her fate. Throughout this period, she lived in constant fear that the police would come to her home and send her back to prison. Those fears materialized in May of 1975, when the New York State Supreme Court confirmed there was insufficient evidence proving that her son was murdered but upheld the conviction for her daughter's murder. History repeats itself. Alice Crimmins was sent back to prison once more.

Throughout her periods of incarceration, those who knew her described Alice Crimmins as "a model inmate." In Bedford Hills, she met Sister Elaine Roulet, a Catholic nun who volunteered in the prison. Sister Elaine was an institution in Bedford Hills and beyond. Until her death in 2020, she devoted her time to helping incarcerated women, especially mothers separated from their children. Her most important project was opening the Children's Center in the prison, so inmates who were mothers could spend time with their children. This unique model was later replicated in other prisons.

Sister Elaine took a liking to Alice. She hired her as a secretary for her charity work, and Alice became eligible for a work-release program in 1976, thanks, in part, to Sister Elaine's support. She worked outside the prison during the day, then would go back in the evenings to spend her nights in the facility. In a letter of recommendation, the nun praised her professionalism and empathy. "I'm not used to writing for a woman, but I'm convinced that she should be granted parole." Alice Crimmins also earned the right to weekend furloughs.

That same year, she was transferred to the Parkside Correctional Facility in Harlem, to be closer to the Catholic thrift shop, where she worked two days a week. She had to be back by 8:00 P.M. on weekdays. One evening, a few minutes before the hour, she was spotted stepping out of a brand-new white Cadillac before making her way back to the prison doors. Her old acquaintance, Anthony Grace, was at the wheel. She'd been spending her weekend furloughs with her old flame. Just as they'd done in the past, the couple would sometimes watch a baseball game from his private box at Shea Stadium. And just as they'd done in the past, the two would soon make headlines yet again.

The yacht docked at a marina in the Bronx belonged to Anthony Grace. But the name painted on the hull made it clear for whom the boat was intended; as a symbol of rebirth, it had been christened *Alicia II*. On Sunday, August 21, 1977, Anthony and Alice were lounging aboard the yacht under the summer sun during one of her furloughs. Photographers spotted the couple, and the following day, the *New York Post* published a photo of Alice on deck wearing a bikini, with the caption "Alice Crimmins should be behind bars!" The paper had been bought a few months earlier by media magnate Rupert Murdoch and had since adopted an increasingly sensationalist approach.

The article provoked an outcry. Reporters were split into two camps. On the one hand, there were those who believed she should be serving time for her crime in a prison cell and not on a yacht. On the other hand, there were some who thought it was time to let her be. But the press would never be done with this case. As they focused their attention on Alice Crimmins, the media uncovered new, unpublished information. While on furlough one month earlier, in July of 1977, Alice had remarried. Under the cover of secrecy, without any pomp and circumstance, she had signed her name in a lawyer's office. Alice would now go by Alice Grace.

They'd been seeing each other for years. In 1973, during a temporary release from prison, Alice Crimmins had moved in with Anthony Grace in the Beechhurst neighborhood of northern Queens, two blocks from the apartment she'd shared with Eddie Crimmins after her children's death. Two years later, when she was back behind bars, there were four people on the list of visitors allowed to see Alice Crimmins: her mother, her brother, her sister-in-law, and Anthony Grace. He came by every Sunday with cigarettes and news from the outside world.

And he fought to support her bid for parole. In 1976, he wrote a letter to the probation board, stating, "The eleven years that have gone by since the children's death have left deep scars in Alice. Her health declined and, with the loss of her children, something went out in her. Yet, despite the trials, she tries to be as comforting and loving as possible toward others." He told the board about their plans to get married and to build a life together, adding, "Mrs. Crimmins, despite everything that has happened, is not an angry person. She has no aggression or desire for revenge. She is calm, kind, and understanding."

Her parole application was denied, but the couple still formalized their union while she was on furlough. In July of 1977, thirteen years after they first met, Anthony Grace and Alice Crimmins became husband and wife.

❖

After the second trial, Anthony Grace's lucky star had begun to fade. In the early 1970s, his name was yet again associated with the Mafia. Once more, it was because of Alice's other former lover, Joseph Rorech. On September 1, 1971, Rorech was arrested by the New Haven, Connecticut, police for issuing a counterfeit check worth sixteen dollars and fifteen cents. The FBI was quick to take over this case . . . and the suspect. Rorech had been on the run for months, as he was wanted for tax fraud.

But the immunity he'd been promised didn't last long. As he prepared to make a getaway, Rorech contacted journalist George Carpozi Jr., who was writing a book about the case. They made a plan to meet at John F. Kennedy Airport, so Rorech could share information. He told Carpozi that some of the leads he'd given the district attorney hadn't been pursued and Rorech figured it was because they involved high-ranking people.

He set the scene. It had all started at the 1964 Democratic National Convention in Atlantic City. Anthony Grace and Alice Crimmins had traveled there on his yacht. At the event, she'd allegedly played matchmaker for a few of her friends and a prominent politician, *a married man*. This was a scandal waiting to happen, and the infidelities were bound to be made public during the custody hearing for the Crimmins children; the revelations would ruin this politician's career.

There was only one way for Alice to protect him—she had to get rid of the children. According to Rorech, the crimes had therefore been premeditated; the children's mother had agreed to take care of it, but she had lost her nerve after strangling Missy. "After all, she loved her son more than her daughter," he explained.

This is when one of Anthony Grace's henchmen, Colabella, was asked to step in and take care of things. Rorech was insistent. This case was, above all, a story about bigwigs with Mafia connections. He also believed one of Sonny Franzese's men—someone in the Colombo clan, one of the New York City Mafia's "Five Families"—had blackmailed Anthony Grace before big boss Joseph "Joe" Colombo himself had told the underling to leave Grace alone. Carpozi was dubious. Wouldn't an investigation into the murders of two children draw far more attention than a mere custody hearing? And if the point was to avoid a court case, why not kill the father?

Still, Carpozi's book, *Ordeal by Trial: The Alice Crimmins Case*, does include this story. The book even ends on it. The tall tale was just enough to pour a little more oil over the fire keeping rumors alive, and it fueled suspicions about Anthony Grace's involvement.

His marriage to Alice Crimmins brought all the theories back to life. One hypothesis flourished: The couple had gotten married to protect a secret because, under the law, a married person could not testify against their spouse. An official union would thus protect both accomplices from being called to testify against each other. Alice Crimmins's critics were certain the wedding had been kept quiet because the newlyweds had something to hide. In fact, before the first trial, Grace had told the cops that he would never marry this "proficient tart." In an interrogation, he had allegedly said, "I told her several times that she should go back to her husband, that she was young. I figured she'd eventually end up on the street."

To this day, Dr. Michael Baden, who participated in the children's autopsy, finds the whole story ironic. "It's always been interesting to me how these things turned out. She grew up very poor and ended up marrying a very rich fellow, after her kids died. Given her prior life, she turned out much better than if she'd just stayed in Queens with her children and nothing went wrong. Nobody ever went after the person who was with her that night."

From a distance, Baden followed Anthony Grace's career, his name appearing twice in the press over the following decades, once for tax evasion and once more in 1990. One newspaper was claiming that, in exchange for contracts, one of his companies, Quality Concrete, had paid mobsters two or three dollars for each yard of road covered in cement.

On September 10, 1977, reporters crossed Alice's path one last time. She was not allowed to leave New York State, could not drive a car without authorization, and had to report to her parole officer on a regular basis, but her parole application had finally been accepted. On the day she was released, thirty reporters gathered by the front gates of the correctional facility in Harlem. As they waited, a gray sedan rounded the corner, and through the back windshield, they caught a glimpse of Alice as she eluded them. She had slipped out through a back door, without a word and without even looking at them.

In the next day's paper, a reporter predicted the now thirty-seven-year-old woman would soon "fade into oblivion" and become "as invisible as possible for a woman in a Cadillac and furs." This turned out to be true. In the 1980s, Alice changed her name in a final attempt to be forgotten at long last, leaving behind her three past identities: Alice Burke, Alice Crimmins, and Alice Grace. As journalist Irene Cornell stated, "From that moment on, she boarded her yacht and disappeared into the wild."

With her name no longer scrawled in detectives' notebooks, or listed in lawyers' calendars, the press let her be, and she became a kind of fictional character. The first novel inspired by her story was published in 1975, when she was sent back to prison in Bedford Hills. *Where Are the Children?* was written by a little-known author at the time, called Mary Higgins Clark. The book was based on stories she'd read in the newspapers and would eventually become her first bestseller. Two years later, novelist Dorothy Uhnak published *The Investigation*. She was a retired police-woman who had served in the New York police force until 1967 and who claimed that she "knew nothing about Alice Crimmins." Yet the similarities between her book and the case are troubling. Audiovisual rights to the novel later sold for 1.6 million dollars.

Since then, Alice Crimmins's story has regularly resurfaced in cinemas, on theater stages, and in bookstores. The last time was in 2016, when author Emma Flint published a novel called *Little Deaths*. Reading the back jacket, it's easy to swap Ruth Malone's name for Alice Crimmins. It's the story of a single mother from Queens who looks like a Hollywood star and who, on an ordinary summer morning, notices her two children have disappeared. She is soon accused of their murders.

13
The Bronx Neighbors

Summer 1964, one year before the night of the crime.

On June 25, police detective John Echevarria and a colleague checked in on a building in the Bronx, just a stone's throw from Crotona Park. It was a standard visit, almost routine, in response to a call the local precinct had received regarding a neighborhood dispute. But the situation quickly got out of hand. The officers were greeted by Carmen Sierra, age fifty-three, and one of her sons. Things became heated. Her son rushed the policemen, ready to fight. His mother grabbed a knife and almost took out Echevarria's eye. Echevarria drew his gun, aimed at Carmen Sierra. He took the shot. A fatal blow. Carmen Sierra was struck in the stomach, fell to the ground, and bled out in minutes. She was driven to the morgue, and her son was taken into police custody.

In a photo published in the next day's newspaper, the detective is crouching, his face covered in blood, with a gash beside one eye. His arm hangs limp, still holding the knife, while Carmen Sierra lies prone at his feet. A blanket covers most of her body, except her head and short brown hair.

The building's super, Mrs. F., had called the police when Carmen Sierra had threatened to kill one of the neighbors. Her sons never forgave the super for ratting out their mother. In their minds, this tragedy was her fault, and they were out for revenge. They warned Mrs. F. that because she had caused their mother's death, they would attack her family in retribution. The authorities took the threat seriously and placed the F. family under witness protection. Their new home was in Kew Gardens Hills, Queens.

The F. family moved from one building to another, before eventually settling down a few streets away from Alice Crimmins. They thought they were safe when, one year after the tragedy, they received a strange letter. It had been mailed to their previous address in the same neighborhood, then forwarded by the postal service to their new home. Inside the envelope was a funeral card on which someone had written Carmen Sierra's name, the date of her death, and the address of the company that had organized her funeral. Despite all their precautions, Mrs. F.'s family had been spotted in the neighborhood and continued to live under threat.

When the Crimmins children were found dead less than a month later, the F. spouses were convinced their family had been targeted that night. They couldn't help but notice the coincidences: They also had several children, two of whom were the same age and sex as Eddie and Missy. Both families lived on the ground floor. Alice Crimmins and Mrs. F. even had some physical traits in common. Later, they found out another family in Alice Crimmins's building had the same last name as the F. family. What if the kidnappers, in trying to locate Mrs. F.'s exact address, had simply gone after the wrong target?

On August 5, 1965, Mrs. F. went to the police station to show investigators the obituary notice and tell her story. The detectives told her they would keep in touch, but she never heard from them again and didn't press the matter. After all, it was best to avoid unnecessary exposure. She kept a low profile and watched the first trial unfold in the media, feeling powerless. But as the years went by, she continued to sense her family was in danger, being stalked. In 1970, a "young man with brown hair in an old gray car" even tried to kidnap one of her children.

When the second Crimmins trial began, she could no longer keep quiet. She confided in an acquaintance who worked for the New York State government. He put her in touch with the judge presiding over the case, who then referred her to Assistant District Attorney Thomas Demakos. When she met with him, Gerard Piering was also present. The detective told Mrs. F. that the NYPD had already looked into her story and asked her to "drop it." He assured her the update had been passed along to the defense.

But that was a lie. During the second trial, the defense attorneys were given myriad documents pointing to all kinds of leads, even a telegram stating that the trial should be stopped immediately "in the name of a revelation from God." But they were never told about Mrs. F. and only learned of her and her story much later, too late. Meanwhile, tired of fighting, Mrs. F. asked the police to give her back the funeral card she had turned over to them in 1965. It was never returned to her.

Is this story plausible? In the streets of Kew Gardens Hills, where the red-brick buildings all look alike, could the Crimmins children really have been abducted and then killed by mistake? It is hard to know if this lead had any substance because police never pursued it in earnest. The same is true for other leads.

For instance, two weeks after the double homicide, a teenager from Queens was found dead in the basement of his building. He had used a twelve-gauge shotgun with a twenty-four-inch barrel to shoot himself in the head. Investigators deemed the death "accidental," even though it was theoretically impossible for someone to accidentally shoot themselves in the head with such a long gun. The detectives may have had good reason to cover up the suicide. Right before his death, the young man had confided in two people, one of his teachers and a priest, and told them that he was "responsible for the deaths of the Crimmins children." Incidentally, this teenager was the son of a Queens policeman. Whether his confession was true or not, the fact remains that investigators never looked into this lead. They likely sought to avoid dragging a colleague into the scandal.

There is also the woman who said she'd seen a man standing in front of the children's window on the night of the crime. He was tall, wearing light brown pants and a black T-shirt, the same clothes Eddie Crimmins was wearing that night. The witness had spoken with Phil Brady, the only police officer who had doubts as to Alice

Crimmins's guilt. But he went no further with this information, as the witness was living off social assistance and occasionally engaged in prostitution. Brady knew all too well that no jury would take her testimony seriously.

Today, William Erlbaum no longer has any reason to defend Alice Crimmins. Although he was her lawyer during the second trial, it's been decades since he represented her. They crossed paths a few times after she finished serving her sentence and then lost sight of each other. After working for seventeen years as a lawyer in Queens, he became a criminal court judge and made his way up the ranks, all the way to the highest court in the state: the New York Supreme Court. Then came retirement.

And while he may have hung up his judge's robe and put his files into storage, two cases continue to haunt him to this day. "Alice Crimmins was framed," he says. "I worked for nearly sixty years in the legal world, and in my entire career, I have used the term 'framed' for only two clients: her and Alvin Mitchell." At the age of eighteen, Alvin Mitchell was sentenced to twelve years in prison for killing fifteen-year-old Barbara Kralik on July

20, 1963, based on a confession he claimed had been given under duress. The guilty verdict was handed up even though the victim had told a different story before dying of her injuries, and even after another man confessed, in great detail, to committing the murder.

"Alvin Mitchell and Alice Crimmins were prosecuted in the same era by the same Queens District Attorney's Office during a time of great cynicism, ruthlessness, remorselessness, limited consciousness, self-indulgence, and careerist opportunism, which pervaded the whole institution," estimates William Erlbaum. "The prevailing prosecutorial culture in Queens was palpably toxic."

In his book, Ken Gross claims that Assistant District Attorney Anthony Lombardino, who led the prosecution in Alice Crimmins's first trial, told him a few years later, "I don't know if she did it. It seems unlikely. I can't believe the story I told the jury." Lombardino has always denied the allegation. A former member of the prosecution in the second trial also admitted to the press, in 1995, that none of them had ever really sought to determine Alice Crimmins's motive.

The Crimmins case has long haunted the New York courts. One former judge, who wishes to remain anonymous, commented that "to crimmins" has become a verb in the New York legal jargon. In what context? "Crimminsing a case means sweeping mistakes made by the prosecutor or the police under the rug, to convict an innocent person."

THE OTHER
DISAPPEARANCE

14

A Few Drops of Blood

Just south of Manhattan is a neighborhood that seems to exist in a different era, out of step with the modern city surrounding it. Near the Chambers Street subway station, historic buildings stand tall, as monumental as the judicial and government operations unfolding within them. In the middle of this court district, at 31 Chambers Street, a seven-story building is particularly unknown and goes unnoticed by passersby.

Yet a treasure lies within its walls: This building holds the memories of an entire city. At the entrance, three massive arched doors guard the marble-clad main lobby of the New York City Department of Records. Inside, in a quasireligious silence, men and women search for answers to questions that haunt them. They seek genealogical information, old land records, and news articles from days past. For hours, they sit focused, immersing themselves in giant ledgers with yellowed pages that are turning to dust or pore over microfilms lit by aging equipment.

One employee is busy retrieving the records we requested from obscure basements. He'll need a cart to transport all the Alice Crimmins case files. In total, there are five cardboard boxes containing most of the minutes, statements, appeals procedures, and anonymous letters. Before disappearing back into the maze of aisles, he points to the largest box and says, "Don't open that one right away. First, look over the other files. Some visitors cry when they open that box."

The box is labeled, simply, "Physical evidence." Inside, each item is carefully wrapped in tissue paper. Viewing evidence is an ordinary procedure here. The Department of Records contains evidence from the city's greatest criminal cases . . . at least those that were solved. In a box stored in the basement, likely wrapped in the same tissue paper, lies another relic from one of New York's most infamous crimes: a bullet that took Malcolm X's life.

In the physical evidence box for the Crimmins case, there is a motel key—room number 106—along with several address books and Alice Crimmins's calendar from 1965. In an elegant, small wooden box, microscope slides have been meticulously stacked. They contain drops of blood, with a classification system that only investigators seem to be able to decipher. Another glass slide contains hair found on little Missy's body, a precious clue. At the bottom of the box, there are more tangible memories of the children, like school notebooks. This is where Eddie Jr. drew his first letters, then his first words: "Missy. Dog. Missy. Dog. Cat." One of the children drew round, smiling people and a pig, also smiling, with a crested hairdo. Many pages are still empty. These are the ones the children never got to fill out. And this is all there is left to get to know the Crimmins children. Shortly after their murders, the story became the "Alice Crimmins case," and the two victims were relegated to the shadows.

Lastly, in a large manila envelope, is the item that brings some of the rare visitors to tears. The evidence is faded, washed out by the half century that has passed since the crimes were committed. The fabric is rough and tattered, the elastic waistband stretched out. But they are brutally tangible, real, palpable. The clothes are there before our eyes: the pajama pants and underwear that Missy was wearing when she was found and the pajama top that was tied around her neck. The fabric features an

innocent pattern, little stagecoaches and carts, the kind
that would feed a young child's imagination, promising
adventure and play.

A few blue stains and darker spots on the top could be
from dirt but leave us wondering if they might be dried
blood. They are a reminder of the violent reality of the
crime and bring about a sudden realization—anyone can
handle these clothes. There isn't even a formal requirement
that visitors wear gloves. If the pajama top, bottoms, and
underwear ever held a tiny clue, an element of DNA from
which modern science could draw an answer, it's too late
now. The clothing has long been contaminated.

All that is left are these slides, a few drops of blood
and hairs that have never been tied to a suspect. And how
long will they last? At one point, the box containing the
physical evidence was temporarily lost in the Department of Records, misplaced, engulfed in the clutter of
the city's history. It took weeks to find it. The very last
pieces of evidence have either disappeared already or may
soon vanish. Will we ever be able to put the puzzle back
together? Ken Gross finds this question irritating: "The
fact that we can't live with a mystery, it's our fault. But
what difference does it make? We will never know. There
are some things that are an eternal mystery. It could have
been anybody. It could have been the husband, a prowler,

there were so many possibilities. The least of which was Alice Crimmins. I mean, imagine her strangling her children, it's not possible to imagine. There are some things that are never solved."

Perhaps some elements of the puzzle are still dormant, squirreled away in a basement somewhere or in the depths of someone's memory. There must be someone out there who kept a secret that could have shed a different light on the case. But few of the people involved in the case are still alive. The central figures have nearly all died, perhaps carrying a small part of the truth to their graves.

Their relatives and descendants seem to have maintained the silence. Some "don't remember anything," while others hang up when we call them. Some people reluctantly decide to speak, then suddenly recant their statement. They deliver implied messages, letting us read between the lines as they cast a shadow of doubt over a potential guilty party, then forever retreat back into their shell. They leave behind rumors, lies, and doubts like a trail of slime. It's as though those connected to the tragedy were overwhelmed by their own destiny and hoped to bury, as quickly as possible, the trauma that the case had caused them.

We probably will never know what to call the Crimmins case: a terrible coincidence, a legal conspiracy, or an ordinary family drama that grew into something far greater? The people most closely related to the case left the next generations with only questions and a haze of mystery.

In New York, some traces of the Crimmins case still remain. Kew Gardens Hills, in Queens, seems to be frozen in time. Since the 1960s, little has changed, save a few details: The delivery drivers who once left bottles of milk on neighborhood stoops have been replaced by an endless parade of Amazon vans and their packages, safely tucked away in building foyers. At the corner of the apartment building where Alice Crimmins and her children once lived, a camera now records people as they come and go. The window to Eddie and Missy's bedroom no longer opens. Instead, an aging air-conditioning unit now sits in the frame, like a bulwark against the outside world.

Nearby, in the Bronx, the St. Raymond cemetery stretches out as far as the eye can see. More than half a million bodies have come to rest in this place. Many of these people's destinies are so diametrically opposed that only a city like New York could bring them together in one resting place. Today, the cemetery is home to singer Billie Holiday, three-time boxing world champion Héctor Camacho, and Irish American gangster Vincent "Mad Dog" Coll.

In this labyrinth, on a lawn that stretches out in front of the reception, in the middle of a row of headstones, someone has left a small sculpted shell at the base of a sober gray headstone. The shell is heart-shaped, with a cherub sleeping in its nook. Three family members have come to rest beneath the shell, all with the last name Crimmins: "beloved son," Edmond Michael "Eddie"; "beloved daughter," Alice Marie "Missy"; and with them, Edmund, "loving husband and father."

15

Florida, Summer 2022

Mary Higgins Clark once shared this story in an interview.* While she was giving a lecture in Florida, a reader told her Alice Crimmins's yacht was docked right next door. At the time, Clark didn't try to use the strange coincidence to meet the woman who had inspired the heroine in her first bestseller. It would have been "too strange." Clark, who died in 2020, provided no date and no precise location in the story, but the author shared one key detail: It happened in the Keys.

---

* Interview by American journalist Sarah Weinman.

The Keys.

Below the mainland of South Florida, a string of islands is connected by a single road that seems to float on the water. This archipelago separates the Atlantic Ocean from the waters of the Gulf of Mexico. When arriving from the north, the first island is Key Largo. From that point, it's a two-and-a-half-hour drive to Key West, at the southern tip.

Like any American city, Key Largo has a pub, where retirees come to sip a beer at eleven o'clock in the morning. This one is the Caribbean Club. A classic beach shack built right on the ocean, the bar emanates a deep nostalgia for a bygone era in this archipelago. From behind the bar, Cathy, who is practically an institution at the Caribbean Club, swears she sees everything. Sure, hordes of people pass through the Keys every year, but few drop an anchor long enough to be noticed. So if a Mary Higgins Clark fan had once spotted *Alicia II* in the area, the boat had likely been there for a while. Cathy "knows everyone." But not Alice Crimmins. Not under any of her names. And the boat? Doesn't ring a bell either.

She refers us to Dan, a mechanic who works on yachts. Skin weathered by ocean spray and years spent in the sun, with a thick beard and hardened eyes, Dan has worked on all the boats in the area for years. If *Alicia II* had been parked here, he would have remembered. But it doesn't ring a bell with him either. At the local history museum, in the village of Islamorada, no one recognizes the name.

Two surprises lay in this small three-room building: a massive lobster living in an aquarium and a full wall dedicated to the fishing exploits of George Bush Sr. A few passionate historians jealously guard these treasures from the past. *Alicia II*? A couple of New Yorkers who came to quietly drop an anchor far from prying eyes? They promise to pore over the archives and contact some of the older residents in the area. Their answer comes back a few days later: nothing. In the fishing ports, marinas, and yacht clubs that dot the one-hundred-mile-long highway connecting the Keys, there is not a single trace of Alice Crimmins, nor her boat.

Still, the last traces of the Crimmins case are, in fact, located in Florida. Joseph Rorech seems to be the only central figure in this case who did not spend a slice of his life in these parts. One of his distant relatives told us that once the case had cooled down, Rorech spent some time behind bars, but she's not exactly sure in which prison. There's no mention of him in the New York State prison archives to confirm the statement. Nothing in the prison records from the National Archives either, as criminal records are no longer available thirty years after a prisoner's release.

The only sure thing about Rorech is this: After repeatedly incriminating Alice Crimmins during her two trials, he remarried and had another child. The seven children from his first marriage never spoke to him again, and he died relatively isolated in 2006.

But aside from Rorech, everyone else made their way to the southern tip of the country.

Lee County, Southwest Florida: Gerard Piering. Died in 2002. A decade after leaving the police force in 1977, Piering settled in the area. He filled his retirement years with his two greatest loves: playing golf and visiting Disney World with his grandchildren. A trace of him can be found in letters to the editor of a local newspaper, published in the late 1990s. He rails against a criminal who got out of a prison sentence, and true to his conservative obsessions, concludes with "Another victory for our progressive lawyers who weep for this scum of the earth. Between the ACLU, all the left-wing lawyers and the press, things are not going well. Wake up, oh America!"

Broward County, North Miami: Sophie Earomirski. Died in 2009. The last time her name appeared in the press was in 1991, when she spoke about a tragedy that struck her family. Her grandson had been playing on a construction site when the tunnel he had dug there collapsed onto him. He was buried alive. "This should never have happened to a child. Nothing is done to protect children in this area," she protested.

Lake County, north of Orlando: Eddie Crimmins. Died in 2012. The children's father moved in with his new wife. She's the person who, upon his death, had an epitaph etched onto the Crimminses' headstone in the Bronx: "Loving husband and father."

A rational way to explain how their fates converged in Florida might be to say that all those involved in the case ended up fleeing the North, with its taxes and gray landscapes. A kind of predetermined path for any New Yorker who is old and rich enough to spend their retirement in the sun.

But Florida has something else to offer, especially in the southernmost reaches. When people move to this last piece of American wilderness, it's never purely happenstance. Built on swampland, Florida is in constant motion, changing and malleable. It's as though the people living on this land can keep taking on new shapes, reinventing themselves. In this place, you can give yourself one last chance. Or disappear into its deepest recesses and let the world forget who you once were.

The sky is milky, the sun beating down, the air humid. A typical early summer day in Florida—stifling. On the beach, the sand burns bare feet as soon as the sun is up. Palm leaves hang stubbornly motionless, like the few early morning visitors, frozen in their lawn chairs. They seem to be desperately waiting for a sea breeze to float up off the Atlantic and set them in motion, but they know full well the weather won't offer any respite and the day will only grow warmer, heavier.

In this small seaside town somewhere in southern Florida, the waterfront is particularly busy. Apartments with an ocean view sell for at least one million. Buyers are all wealthy retirees. One of the buildings, set back from the road, rivals the luxury of neighboring complexes. On the beach side, elegant, glazed balconies rise up to thirteen stories. Residents can access the sea right from the ground floor or, if they prefer to keep to themselves within the development, they can enjoy the private pool and jacuzzi. On the street side, parking lots are filled with Porsches, Bentleys, and other luxury cars. This is supposedly where Alice Crimmins lives today.

To find her, I had to spend days cross-referencing information online, details that often turned out to be false. But eventually, I landed on a credible lead pointing to her new identity. The leak came from her voter registration in Florida. Ironically, this woman whose trip to the Democratic National Convention caused such a stir, and who was hounded like the devil by most conservatives in her younger days, is now a registered Republican.

In one of her interviews with Ken Gross, conducted between prison stints, Alice Crimmins recounted the effects of her first arrest in 1967, which had been carried out in the parking lot in front of her building. "I have always been a very happy-go-lucky person. I'd always have my door open, have people dropping in. I'd always walk out with a kind of expectation. A new day; a new beginning. It was always an invigorating thing, to walk outdoors on a bright summer day. Until that day, that is. I've never been able to walk out without looking in both directions since. I never open my door anymore unless I ask who it is."

Fifty years later, these words come to mind as I step into the luxurious residence. The grand marble lobby is guarded by cameras and zealous concierges. They form a blockade. No one can continue down the hall without an invitation. The guards reluctantly confirm that Alice Crimmins does indeed live in this building. But she's out. Has she been away for a few hours, a few days? They fall back into a silence befitting their profession. We can leave her a message, but cannot knock on her door.

Did Detective Piering know that nothing but a vast swamp stood between him and the woman who had haunted him throughout the biggest case of his career? The two enemies had each set up camp on opposite coasts of this southern state, each solidly anchored to their own shoreline and their own version of events. All Piering would have had to do was take a map of Florida and draw a straight line across the middle of the state and it would have brought him straight to Alice Crimmins.

Despite the circumstances—or despite herself?— Alice Crimmins left a window open into her life: her Facebook page. Dozens of posts and photos depict her daily life, revealing what cannot be seen from the beach: the inside of her apartment, which is just as extravagant as the facade. The few rare photos of her show an eighty-four-year-old woman. Her hair is the same shade of fiery red she wore in her youth, and her cheekbones have been enhanced, perhaps surgically.

What else? She never had another child. She was married to Anthony Grace until his death in 1998. She still has a close relationship with her brother and dotes on her grandnephews. She still travels to the Caribbean and is still crazy about dogs, like her Papillon spaniel, the star of her Facebook page and her life. When she celebrated her most recent birthday in style at a local restaurant, the moment was immortalized with a photo of the dog sitting in a baby carriage and wearing a faux diamond tiara. His nickname is only one letter off from her daughter's name.

For the rest, Alice Crimmins, like most people of her generation, uses the social network to communicate via heart-shaped stickers and shared viral posts. Most seem insignificant. Others seem to resonate with her story. Like the photo of a pink rose she posted in 2021, with a caption that is strangely reminiscent of the words Anthony Grace had written to support her parole application: "All humans hide something. Rare women like you aren't just born strong, they're made strong by what they've been through. You are like a diamond—unbreakable. You have seen a lot of darkness in your life, but decided to never allow your demons to turn you cruel. You choose to love with your whole heart." The post got two likes and this comment from a friend: "Wow this so sounds like you!"

Deep in the Everglades grows one of the rarest flowers in the world. The ghost orchid blooms for only one week a year. White and ethereal, the delicate flowers can be hard to spot, and for enthusiasts who would go to great lengths to see them, they are an obsession. Some fanatics are willing to risk their lives to see the orchid bloom, wading for hours in swamps rife with snakes and alligators.

Trying to catch a glimpse of Alice Crimmins in Florida requires a similar approach. You have to get up early, in the hopes that she will walk her dog in front of her home. Street side? Sea side? A day goes by. Two days. Three days. Time drags on, and you are lulled by the sound of waves lapping at pilings. In front of her building, the bus stop offers a sheltered view of the residents as they come and go. Over the course of three days, more iguanas than buses will pass by this shelter. On her balcony, there is nothing but stillness. Windows and blinds don't move an inch. She is so close, yet inaccessible.

There is still one last way to contact her. Some phone numbers are listed online under her current last name, which is quite common in the United States. First, there are the wrong numbers, unassigned numbers, men with a Spanish accent . . . and then suddenly, on an answering machine, we hear her unmistakable voice, delicate with a slow cadence. Alice Crimmins screens her calls. Her answering machine raises yet another barricade. Just as she never responded to my letter, she will never reply to messages left on her answering machine, nor to text messages. At this point, she must be aware that we have been trying to reach her. But in her ivory tower, she remains a mirage. Alice Crimmins is nowhere to be seen. She is alone, shrouded in mystery, carrying either a heavy secret or questions that will forever go unanswered.

A few days after calls, texts, and notes left with her concierge in Florida, Alice Crimmins publishes a new post on her Facebook page, her first one in weeks. It's a picture of her dog, half hidden in a plaid blanket on the couch, in a living room that seems to be hers. The caption, either a hidden message or a sheer coincidence, reads:

"Can you find me?"

APPENDICES

NEW YORK CITY AND LONG ISLAND

LONG ISLAND

BRONX

QUEENS

MANHATTAN

BROOKLYN

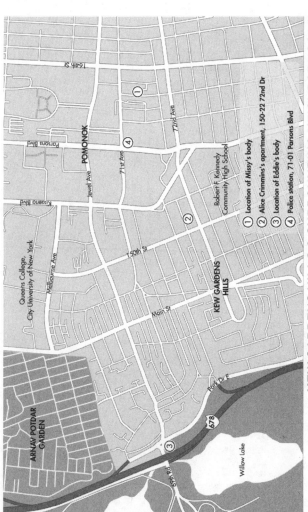

KEW GARDENS HILLS & SURROUNDING NEIGHBORHOODS

① Location of Missy's body
② Alice Crimmins's apartment, 150-22 72nd Dr
③ Location of Eddie's body
④ Police station, 71-01 Parsons Blvd

Timeline

November 1958: Alice and Eddie Crimmins are married.

October 17, 1959: Eddie Crimmins Jr. is born.

October 24, 1960: Alice "Missy" Crimmins is born.

July 20, 1963: Barbara Kralik is murdered in Queens.

November 22, 1963: John Fitzgerald Kennedy is assassinated in Dallas.

February 1964: Alice and Eddie Crimmins separate.

1964: Alice Crimmins and Anthony Grace meet in a Queens bar.

March 13, 1964: Kitty Genovese is murdered in Kew Gardens.

June 25, 1964: In the Bronx, a neighborhood argument escalates, Carmen Sierra is killed by a detective.

August 1964: Alice Crimmins and Anthony Grace attend the Democratic National Convention in Atlantic City.

Late January 1965: Anthony Grace and Alice Crimmins go on a Caribbean cruise.

February 21, 1965: Malcolm X is assassinated in Manhattan.

May 1965: Michael Burke, Alice Crimmins's father, dies.

End of June 1965: Eddie Crimmins officially requests custody of the children.

Night of July 13 to 14, 1965: The Crimmins children go missing.

July 14, 1965: Missy's body is found.

July 19, 1965: Eddie's body is found.

July 20, 1965: Original date scheduled for the child custody hearing.

End of Summer 1965: Alice and Eddie Crimmins move in together, in Beechhurst, Queens.

November 1965: New York City municipal elections are held.

September 22, 1966: Thirteen mob bosses are arrested at the La Stella restaurant in Queens.

November 1966: A grand jury is convened in the Crimmins case.

November 1966: Elections are held for the Queens District Attorney.

End of November 1966: Sophie Earomirski sends her anonymous letter to the police.

September 11, 1967: Alice Crimmins is indicted by a third grand jury.

September 12, 1967: Alice Crimmins is arrested.

1968: The women's liberation movement begins in the United States.

April 4, 1968: Martin Luther King is assassinated.

May 1968: Alice Crimmins's first trial is held.

May 27, 1968: Alice Crimmins receives her first conviction for the murder of her daughter (sentence: five to twenty years in prison).

September 5, 1968: Alice Crimmins is released from prison after her attorneys appeal her verdict.

September 9, 1968: Protests are held at the Miss America pageant in Atlantic City.

January 20, 1969: Richard Nixon is elected president of the United States.

August 1969: Woodstock.

December 1969: The New York Supreme Court overturns the verdict; Alice Crimmins will be retried.

Fall 1970: Alice and Eddie Crimmins get a divorce.

1970: Anthony Grace's wife dies.

1971: *The Trials of Alice Crimmins* is released by Women Make Movies.

March 15, 1971: The second trial of Alice Crimmins begins.

April 23, 1971: Alice Crimmins is convicted of the murder of her daughter (sentence: five to twenty years in prison) and the murder of her son (sentence: life in prison).

September 1971: Joseph Rorech is arrested in Connecticut.

September 1971: Attica Prison riot.

January 22, 1973: Abortion is legalized in the United States.

May 1973: The second verdict is overturned, and Alice Crimmins is released from prison.

1973: Alice Crimmins moves in with Anthony Grace, in Beechhurst, Queens.

August 1974: Mutiny at the Bedford Hills Correctional Facility for Women.

May 1975: The New York Supreme Court upholds the conviction for the murder of Alice Crimmins's daughter, but overturns the conviction for the murder of her son. Alice Crimmins is sent back to prison to serve the rest of her five-to-twenty-year sentence for the murder of her daughter.

1976: Alice Crimmins begins a work-release program.

July 1977: Anthony Grace and Alice Crimmins get married while she is on furlough.

Night of July 13 to 14, 1977: The historic New York City blackout results in a night of rioting.

September 10, 1977: Alice Crimmins is released on parole.

October 22, 1998: Anthony Grace dies.

June 5, 2002: Gerard Piering dies.

2006: Joseph Rorech dies.

2011: The trial of Casey Anthony begins. She is accused of killing her daughter, Caylee, and becomes the most hated woman in America, with the media comparing her story to that of Alice Crimmins.

2012: Eddie Crimmins dies.

Sources

This book is the result of an extensive documentation process relying on archives, interviews, and investigations from both New York and Florida. The work was carried out in the first half of 2022.

Quotes from Michael Baden, Irene Cornell, Ariel Dougherty, William Erlbaum, and Ken Gross are from interviews conducted by the author. Other quotes are from the books and newspapers listed below.

Books

Carpozi, George, Jr. *Ordeal by Trial: The Alice Crimmins Case*. Walker & Co., 1972.

English, T. J. *The Savage City*. HarperCollins, 2011.

Friedan, Betty. *The Feminine Mystique*. Penguin Classics, 1963.

Gross, Ken. *The Alice Crimmins Case*. Alfred A. Knopf, 1975.

Jones, Ann. *Women Who Kill*. Holt, Rinehart & Winston, 1980.

Orlean, Susan. *The Orchid Thief*. Random House, 1998.

Povich, Lynn. *The Good Girls Revolt*. PublicAffairs, 2012.

Zinn, Howard. *A People's History of the United States: 1492– Present*. Pearson Longman, 2003.

Articles

Borowitz, Albert. "Did Alice Crimmins kill her kids?" *The Daily Beast*, April 11, 2015.

Corrigan, Maureen. "Still unsolved, a child-murder case inspires a gripping new novel." *The Washington Post*, January 15, 2017.

Kassin, Saul M. "The killing of Kitty Genovese: what else does this case tell us?" *Perspective on Psychological Science* 12, no. 3 (2017).

Weinman, Sarah. "Why can't you behave?" Revisiting the Case of Alice Crimmins. *Hazlitt*, July 16, 2015.

Other Sources

Archives of *The New York Times*, the *Daily News*, the *New York Post*, and many newspapers from this era, including *Dyke* magazine, *A Quarterly*, and the *Village Voice* on the August 1974 Bedford Hills rebellion.

Alice Crimmins case files kept at the New York City Department of Records.

Documents regarding Alice Crimmins's life in prison, from the New York State Archives.

Works of Fiction

Flint, Emma. *Little Deaths*. Picador, 2016.

Higgins Clark, Mary. *Where Are the Children?* Simon and Schuster, 1975.

Uhnak, Dorothy. *The Investigation*. Simon and Schuster, 1970.

Acknowledgments

This investigatigation was made possible thanks to the help of valuable sources and the support of my loved ones.

I would especially like to thank four people who met with me in the United States:

–Irene Cornell, for agreeing to share her memories despite the emotional burden left behind by this case.

–William Erlbaum, for his invaluable help.

–Ken Gross, for his work on the case, and for acting as a precious source and a gateway into the thoughts of those who cannot—or no longer wish to—speak today. His dedication is one of the main reasons this case has not been forgotten.

–Sarah Weinman, author of *Scoundrel: How a Convicted Murderer Persuaded the Women Who Loved Him, the Conservative Establishment, and the Courts to Set Him Free*, for all her advice and the documents she shared.

I also wish to thank all those who took the time to dive back into their memories for our interviews:

–Jeffrey Abdale, who attended the 1968 trial.

–Jason Antos, Director of the Queens Historical Society.

–Wendy Antos, a former neighbor of Alice Crimmins.

–William Aylward, a journalist and actor.

–Dr. Michael Baden, forensic pathologist.

–Ariel Dougherty, cofounder of Women Make Movies, director, and producer.

–Alex Hortis, attorney and author of *The Mob and the City: The Hidden History of How the Mafia Captured New York*, Prometheus, 2014.

–Ann Jones, journalist.

–Wilbur Miller, police historian.

–Lynn Povich, journalist.

–Debra Zimmerman, director at Women Make Movies.

And to all those who spoke with me off the record to help me understand the case and its context, the American legal system, as well as the relatives of the central figures in the case for sharing some of their memories.

And because long-term investigations are never carried out alone, thank you from the bottom of my heart to:

–Elsa and Stéphane, for putting their trust in me.

–My parents, Geneviève and François, for everything.

–Anna, for her strength of character.

–Anne-Laure, Nicolas, Alexis, and Mathieu, for their solidarity in the final stretch.

–Arno and Thomas, for regularly inviting me to visit them in the United States.

–Arthur, Camille, Clara, Clémence, Coline, Laurent, Léa, Manon (and Dirk), Mathieu, Rose, Sabine, the Wonderlands and the Mayi-Tai, and all my friends who supported me throughout the investigation.

–Big Al for this dive into New York (*Go Mets!*).

–Xriss and Mya for their warm welcome and friendship.

–Mark Askins for access to databases.

–Anna Blume, who accompanied me for eleven years and until the end of the writing process.

About the Author

Anaïs Renevier is a French journalist. She began her career in 2011 as a correspondent in Beirut, Lebanon, reporting about the Middle East for multiple international media outlets. As an independent reporter, she now regularly travels across the United States on investigative assignments. She likes to tell the country's story from the perspective of those living at the margins of society. Outside of her work as a journalist, she freelances as a florist and enjoys boxing. She lives in Marseille, France.

CRIME INK PRESENTS

FRANCE'S LEADING TRUE CRIME JOURNALISTS INVESTIGATE AMERICA'S MOST NOTORIOUS CASES — ONE FOR EVERY STATE IN THE UNION.

Each title revisits an infamous crime, replete with all the hard facts and gruesome details, and brings fresh new perspectives to these storied cases. Taken together, the series reveals a dark national legacy, state-by-state, from sea to shining sea . . .

NEW YORK:
THE ALICE CRIMMINS CASE
ANAÏS RENEVIER
TRANSLATED BY LAURIE BENNETT
ISBN: 978-1-61316-629-1
The case that rocked New York City in the summer of '65. Two children disappear and turn up dead. Their beautiful and promiscuous mother is convicted in the court of public opinion . . . but did she commit the crime?

CALIFORNIA:
THE GOLDEN STATE KILLER CASE
WILLIAM THORP
TRANSLATED BY LYNN E. PALERMO
ISBN: 978-1-61316-631-4
For years a methodical killer stalked the shadows of sunny California. Responsible for at least fifty assaults and thirteen murders, an unlikely modern development led to an arrest more than forty years after his reign of terror began.

OHIO:
THE CLEVELAND JOHN DOE CASE
THIBAULT RAISSE
TRANSLATED BY LAURIE BENNETT
ISBN: 978-1-61316-633-8
A body is discovered by police in 2002 . . . but it doesn't match its name. The deceased had assumed a false identity. Who was he really? And what other secrets was he hiding?